Principles of Livestock Breeding

by Sewall Wright

with an introduction by Jackson Chambers

This work contains material that was originally published in 1920.

This publication is within the Public Domain.

This edition is reprinted for educational purposes and in accordance with all applicable Federal Laws.

Introduction Copyright 2017 by Jackson Chambers

Self Reliance Books

Get more historic titles on animal and stock breeding, gardening and old fashioned skills by visiting us at:

http://selfreliancebooks.blogspot.com/

Introduction

I am pleased to present yet another title on the Principles of Animal Breeding.

This volume is entitled "Principles of Livestock Breeding" and was published in 1920.

The work is in the Public Domain and is re-printed here in accordance with Federal Laws.

As with all reprinted books of this age that are intended to perfectly reproduce the original edition, considerable pains and effort had to be undertaken to correct fading and sometimes outright damage to existing proofs of this title. At times, this task is quite monumental, requiring an almost total "rebuilding" of some pages from digital proofs of multiple copies. Despite this, imperfections still sometimes exist in the final proof and may detract from the visual appearance of the text.

I hope you enjoy reading this book as much as I enjoyed making it available to readers again.

Jackson Chambers

UNITED STATES DEPARTMENT OF AGRICULTURE

BULLETIN No. 905

Contribution from the Bureau of Animal Industry

JOHN R. MOHLER, Chief

Washington, D. C. ▼ December 8, 1920

PRINCIPLES OF LIVESTOCK BREEDING.

By SEWALL WRIGHT,
Senior Animal Husbandman, Animal Husbandry Division.

CONTENTS.

	Page.		Page.
Evolution of animal breeding	1	Mendelian heredity in livestock—Continued.	
Reproduction	2	Colors of sheep	33
The cell theory	2	Colors and comb shape of poultry	33
The reproductive cells	3	Heredity of form and function in livestock	34
Sexual maturity	4	Relations of theory to practice	34
Frequency of service	5	Equality of inheritance from the sexes	34
The breeding season and œstrous cycle	6	Prepotency	34
The gestation period	7	Variation	36
Fertility	8	Fixation of heredity by selection	37
Hybrids	10	Fixation of heredity by inbreeding	37
The reproductive cells in relation to heredity	11	Isolation of genetic differences by inbreeding	39
General considerations	11	The effect of inbreeding on vigor	40
Modification of heredity	12	Crossbreeding	42
Inheritance of acquired characteristics	13	The system of breeding	42
Telegony	14	The purposes of livestock breeding	42
Maternal impressions	15	Uniformity of type	43
Details of hereditary transmission	15	Crossbreeding for the market	44
Blending and alternative inheritance	15	Improvement	45
Hereditary units	15	Grading up	46
Color and albinism in guinea pigs	16	Methods of selection	47
Mendelian inheritance	18	General considerations	47
The chromosomes and heredity	20	Individual performance and livestock judging	49
Linkage	20		
The determination of sex	23	The breeding record	50
The normal method	23	Pedigrees	50
Sex-linked inheritance	25	The value of purebreds	54
The sex ratio	27	Dairy cattle	54
The freemartin	29	Quality in meat	57
Mendelian heredity in livestock	30	Breeding and soundness in horses	61
Polled cattle	30	Poultry	62
Colors of cattle	30	Satisfaction from pleasing appearance	63
Colors of horses	31	Summary	65
Colors of hogs	32		

EVOLUTION OF ANIMAL BREEDING.

The breeding of domestic animals dates back to remote antiquity, when the most advanced races of the Old World were still on the border line between savagery and barbarism. It far antedates any but the simplest mechanical arts. Yet, while our knowledge of the laws of nature as they apply to machines has reached very great magnitude and complexity, it is comparatively only a few years since the principles of breeding have been more than a collection of unrelated traditional beliefs. The same superstitions on which the shepherds of Asia based their practices at least 30 centuries ago are still widely current, while the one sound principle known to the ancients—selection of the best for breeding stock—is still widely neglected.

The earliest records show that the domestic animals had already become much modified from their wild ancestry. The process of change, however, had probably been exceedingly gradual and has continued so until very recently. A thoroughly self-conscious movement toward improvement of livestock dates back hardly more than a century and a half. Robert Bakewell, of Leicestershire, England, is credited with being the pioneer in this movement.

The breeders of the time of Bakewell suspected him of possessing and concealing special principles of breeding. It is often believed to-day that successful breeders have some mysterious method of which others are ignorant. Instead, the principles of the successful breeder have been exceedingly simple. He isolates and fixes a good type by careful selection and close breeding. If ambitious to take a greater step in advance, he crosses types with characteristics which seem to offer possibilities for a desirable combination and fixes the new ideal by continued selection and close breeding. He brings inferior stock up to a higher level by consistent use of prepotent sires of the same improved type. The difficulty lies not so much in knowing the principles as in applying them. Without skill in feeding and management, the possibilities of the animals can not be brought out in such way as to give a satisfactory basis for selection. Selection of breeding stock, moreover, requires the best judgment in estimating the merits of the animal's own performance, its conformation, ancestry, and previous success as a breeder, and also in giving each of these its due weight. Good judgment, industry, and persistence in following a given aim, as well as knowledge of sound principles, have been the qualities which have made successful breeders.

REPRODUCTION.

THE CELL THEORY.

There could be no clear ideas of breeding until something was known in detail of the processes through which a new individual starts on his career and develops. The most important step in this direction was the discovery that all living organisms are built up of microscopical living units, the cells, with characteristics which do not differ greatly in the most widely different plants and animals. These cells are semifluid bits of living matter, each bounded by a membrane. Each contains within itself a differentiated portion called the nucleus. The details of the structure are brought out by the use of dyes, which are seized upon by certain cell structures and not by others. Thus if an animal of plant tissue is properly preserved and stained with hematoxylin, a dye from logwood, a number of threadlike or rod-shaped bodies, called chromosomes, are made visible in the nucleus of each cell, through their taking on of a dark-blue color.

It has been found that the number of these chromosomes in the cells of each kind of animal or plant is constant, with certain qualifications, one of which will be taken up later. There are, for instance, 40 in swine, 48 in man, 8 in the fruit fly, 20 in corn, and 16 in wheat. A great deal of attention has been devoted to the chromosomes in recent years, as it has been demonstrated that they play an all-important part in heredity and the determination of sex. We shall have occasion to refer to them later.

A study of any rapidly growing part of a young animal soon reveals cells which are in the act of dividing to form two cells. New cells are formed in the body only in this way. The individual begins his career as a single cell. This divides into two, the daughter cells divide, and so on until the trillions of cells of the adult body are produced.

THE REPRODUCTIVE CELLS.

The original single cell, though barely visible to the naked eye, must somehow contain within itself all the potentialities, physical and mental, of the organism into which it is to develop. The characteristics of both the paternal and maternal lines of ancestry must be represented in it. It is, in fact, the product of the fusion between two cells, one a sperm cell furnished by the male parent, and the other an ovum, or egg cell, from the female parent.

The reproductive cells from the two sexes have very different appearances. In mammals, the ovum is a relatively large, spherical cell, just visible to the naked eye. In birds, the yolk of an egg is really a single ovum, distended to an enormous size by food material. The sperm cell is very much smaller and can be seen well only with a high-power microscope. It is something like a tadpole in shape, having a small cell body, containing little but the nucleus, and attached to this a long, whiplike process which beats rapidly while the cell is alive, enabling it to seek out and unite with the large, passive egg cell in the act of fertilization. Enormous numbers of sperm cells are produced by the male, but only one takes part in fertilization. After the first has penetrated the membrane of an egg cell, a change takes place in the latter which prevents the entrance of others.

SEXUAL MATURITY.

Animals reproduce only during the part of their lifetime following sexual maturity and preceding senescence. During this period most of them reproduce only in a certain season of the year, the breeding season, and within this season a given female will breed during only

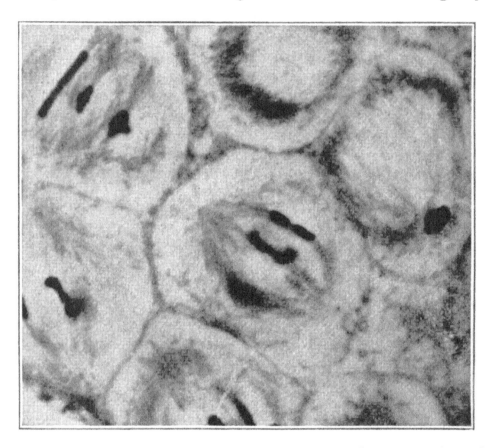

FIG. 1.—A group of dividing reproductive cells from a male grasshopper. The curious spindle-shaped figure, which is characteristic of dividing cells, is clearly brought out. In the formation of the reproductive cells, the chromosomes, which appear solid black in the illustration, come together in pairs around the equator of the spindle, separate and move to opposite poles, forming two nuclei as a preliminary to division of the cell as a whole. Each of the resulting cells has only half the original number of chromosomes. In ordinary cell divisions, each chromosome splits, the halves moving to opposite poles, each of which thus obtains the same number of chromosomes as the original cell. Only a few of the chromosomes are in focus in the picture, which was taken through a high-power microscope. (Courtesy of Dr. E. E. Carothers.)

a very brief period, the period of heat or œstrus. In many cases the œstrous period recurs at definite intervals during the breeding season.

The age of maturity, while in a general way characteristic for a given kind of animal, depends on a great number of factors in individual cases. A warm climate, liberal feeding, and good care in general are conducive to early maturity. There are also hereditary differences. Early sexual maturity is doubtless correlated with the early maturity in growth that has been one of the characteristics for which the domestic animals have been most carefully selected.

Under favorable conditions hogs, sheep, cattle, and horses mature at remarkably early ages. Females usually become mature a little earlier than males under the same conditions, but the difference is not great. Boars and sows have been known to breed as early as 3 months, bulls and heifers at 4 months, rams and ewes at 5 months, and stallions and mares at 12 months. It is not, however, considered advisable to breed animals until some time after sexual maturity has begun, in order to avoid interference with their development. Moreover, the young will not obtain so good a start as they should unless the dam has nearly finished her own growth. It has also been asserted that the offspring of a very young sire are apt to be unthrifty, but there seems to be little evidence for this belief. Sows may usually be bred without harm at about 8 months, permitting their offspring to be born just a year from their own birth. Ewes are often bred at 7 months to lamb at a year, but under ordinary conditions a thrifty flock can not be maintained unless breeding is deferred until a year later. Heifers may usually be bred at 15 months, which means calving at 2 years of age. Most fillies can be bred at 2 years and practically all by 3 years. Limited use of males may be begun at about these same ages.

FREQUENCY OF SERVICE.

The number of females which can be served by a mature male varies greatly under different circumstances. Most care seems to be necessary with the stallion, in which fertility rapidly declines after a number of daily services. Eighty mares is about the limit of the number which should be served by one stallion in a season. With careful handling a single bull may be used with 60 or 70 cows, a single ram with even more than 100 ewes, and a single boar with 30 or 40 sows. Under range conditions the numbers are much less. One bull may run with 20 to 30 cows and one ram with 40 to 70 ewes.

The principal effect of too frequent service on a mature male seems to be temporary sterility. Daily service by a vigorous stallion was found by Lewis, of the Oklahoma experiment station, to be accompanied with a rapid decrease in both the number and vitality of the sperm cells. It is a common belief that fertilization by the weakened sperm cells, formed after excessive service, will result in unthrifty young, but the experimental evidence does not support this view. O. Lloyd-Jones and F. A. Hays, of the Iowa experiment station, made extensive experiments on rabbits to test this question. After too frequent service they found a marked decline in the percentage of pregnancies induced and ultimately a decline in the size of litters, leading to temporary sterility. Microscopical study showed a marked decline in the motility of the sperm cells. Nevertheless, such offspring as were obtained from the late services were in every way as vigorous as those from early services.

Artificial insemination may be mentioned at this point as a practice which is useful in extending the service of a valuable male and in overcoming certain forms of sterility. This practice is especially useful in the case of horses, but has also been used to some extent with cattle and dogs.

THE BREEDING SEASON AND ŒSTROUS CYCLE.

Wild animals generally have a fairly definite breeding season, which in most cases occurs at such a time that the young are born in the spring or summer. The smaller animals, in which the gestation period is very short and which develop rapidly, such as mice, rats, rabbits, and moles, usually have an extended breeding season from early spring through summer; wolves and foxes, with a gestation period of 2 months, breed in winter. Where the gestation period approaches half a year, the breeding season comes in the fall, as in the wild sheep and goats and the Texas armadillo. The bison and most deer, with a longer gestation period, breed late in the summer or early in the fall. There are some curious exceptions, such as bats, whose breeding season is in the fall; the ova remain unfertilized all winter and go through a development lasting 2 months in the spring.

The breeding season has become much obscured or wholly lost in most of the domestic animals. Most breeds of sheep, however, retain the definite fall breeding season and consequent spring lambing season of their wild forbears. The Dorset breed is exceptional in that the ewes will breed in the spring soon after the birth of lambs, conceived in the preceding fall. The sheep of Australia have come to breed at all seasons of the year. Mares come in heat most regularly in the spring and summer and the great majority of the foals are born in the months of April, May, and June after a gestation period of 11 months. Some are born, however, in all months of the year. About 50 per cent of all the calves and pigs are born in the months of March, April, and May. There is a secondary rise in the number of births early in the fall in both cases. Under favorable conditions sows are often bred to produce two litters a year with profit.

During the fall breeding season ewes have a number of periods of heat, each lasting 2 or 3 days and at intervals of 2 to 3 weeks. Mares come in heat normally about 9 days after foaling. The heat period lasts several days and recurs at intervals of 3 or 4 weeks. Cows come in heat from 6 to 8 weeks after calving if suckling the calf, otherwise after 3 or 4 weeks. The heat period is of very brief duration, lasting only a day or less. There is recurrence every 3 weeks. Sows come in heat 3 days after farrowing and again within a week after weaning the pigs. After this there is, as in the other cases, recurrence about every 3 weeks. Both the duration and the time of recurrence seem to vary considerably in different individuals.

THE GESTATION PERIOD.

Normally one or more ripe egg cells are released during the heat period. If fertilization takes place, there is as a rule no recurrence of heat until after the birth of the young. The average length of the gestation period is given below for a number of animals.

Gestation period in animals.

Mare	11 months (340 days).
Jennet	12 months.
Cow	9¼ months (280 days).
Ewe	5 months (150 days).
Goat	5 months.
Sow	4 months (114 days).
Dog	2 months.
Cat	2 months.
Guinea pig	2¼ months (68 days).
Rabbit	1 month (30 days).
Rat	(22 days).
Mouse	(22 days).

The period of incubation in fowls corresponds to the gestation period in animals. The following periods are given for comparison:

Incubation period in fowls.

Ostrich	42 days.
Goose	30 days.
Duck	28 days.
Turkey	28 days.
Guinea fowl	27 days.
Pheasant	23 days.
Domestic fowl	21 days.
Pigeon	18 days.
Canary	13 days.

The gestation and incubation periods are both subject to considerable variation. There seem to be slight breed differences among the domestic animals. Thus, Darwin gives the average period for Southdown sheep as 144 days compared with 150 days for Merinos. The variation among individuals within a breed is, however, more important. Thus, it is about an even chance that a foal will be born between 333 and 347 days after service and there is also an even chance that it will be born outside of these limits. It is an even chance that a calf will be born within 3 or 4 days of the 280th day. With sows it is not quite an even chance that birth comes on the 113th, 114th, or 115th day. The table below gives the most probable day of birth following service on the first day of any month. The date of birth for any other day of service can easily be calculated.

Probable day of birth.

Date of service.	Date of birth of young.			
	Sow.	Ewe.	Cow.	Mare.
Jan. 1	Apr. 25	May 31	Oct. 8	Dec. 7
Feb. 1	May 26	July 1	Nov. 8	Jan. 7
Mar. 1	June 23	July 29	Dec. 6	Feb. 4
Apr. 1	July 24	Aug. 29	Jan. 6	Mar. 7
May 1	Aug. 23	Sept. 28	Feb. 5	Apr. 6
June 1	Sept. 23	Oct. 29	Mar. 8	May 7
July 1	Oct. 23	Nov. 28	Apr. 7	June 6
Aug. 1	Nov. 23	Dec. 29	May 8	July 7
Sept. 1	Dec. 24	Jan. 29	June 8	Aug. 7
Oct. 1	Jan. 23	Feb. 28	July 8	Sept. 6
Nov. 1	Feb. 23	Mar. 31	Aug. 8	Oct. 7
Dec. 1	Mar. 25	Apr. 30	Sept. 7	Nov. 6

FERTILITY.

There are few problems in practical breeding more important than increase in fertility. The losses to livestock farming from failure in fertility have been estimated as enormous. There are two phases of fertility which must be considered—regularity of breeding and number of young at a birth.

In cattle and horses, in which twins are neither common nor desirable, only the first phase is important. It is generally stated that twins are born in about 1 birth in 80 in cattle. Triplets and even larger numbers are born occasionally. The number of twin births in horses is generally stated as much less than in cattle, but a tabulation of 3,000 births taken at random from three recent volumes of the General Stud Book (English Thoroughbreds) yielded 66 cases. However, in 29 cases the foals were slipped, and only 12 of the 132 were born alive. According to this tabulation, twins are born once in 45 births, but only one living horse in more than 200 is born a twin.

Among the factors which affect fertility in both its phases are age, heredity, climate, feeding, and disease. As already noted, hogs, sheep, and cattle begin to become capable of reproduction when less than half a year old and horses at about a year. Fertility is relatively low at first, both in respect to regularity of breeding and the number of young at a birth. There is a rapid rise to a maximum and then a gradual decline.

The productive period usually comes to an end among light horses of both sexes between 20 and 25 years of age. The corresponding ages in heavy horses are 15 to 20 years, in cattle 10 to 15 years, in sheep 7 to 10 years, in hogs 5 to 8 years.

Examples of breeding at much greater ages can, of course, be found. A ewe is recorded as lambing at 19 years of age. As for the maximum length of life, horses are reported to have passed 40 years, cattle 30 years, sheep 20 years.

Chickens hatched early in spring usually begin to lay in from 6 to 8 months, but cases of laying at less than 5 months are on record. The best egg record is usually produced in the first full year of laying. The second and often the third years are nearly as good in the egg breeds. After this the number declines, but laying may continue to the eighth or ninth year.

That heredity is a factor in determining fertility may be seen by comparing the different breeds of hogs and sheep. Among hogs, the bacon breeds, as the Tamworth and the large Yorkshires, have considerably larger litters than the lard breeds. There are differences among the latter. In very extensive tabulations made by G. M. Rommel the average for Poland Chinas was 7.52, compared with 9.26 for Duroc-Jerseys. Averages for the other important lard breeds are intermediate. Among sheep, certain breeds, such as the Dorsets, Oxford Downs, and Shropshires, have twins more frequently than singles under favorable conditions. Southdowns are distinctly less fecund, while among Merinos twins are not common. Within a breed, the number at a birth is determined by such a variety of factors that it is not easy to demonstrate the influence of heredity. Nevertheless it has been shown for Poland China hogs (Rommel and Phillips) and for Shropshire sheep (Rietz and Roberts) that females born in large litters in the former and as twins in the latter have a slight tendency to produce more at a birth than the average.

Differences in fertility appear to be so great among individuals that breeders often look for some outer indication. It is generally believed that strong development of the masculine and feminine types in males and females, respectively, gives a special indication of fertility as well as of general vigor. It is sometimes thought that the fertility of a female is indicated by the number of mammæ. Professor Pearl has shown that this is true in a general way in a comparison of different kinds of mammals. It does not, however, seem to hold to any significant extent within a single species. Thus Alexander Graham Bell was able to increase the number of functional nipples in his flock of sheep from 2 to 6 by careful selection. This change was not accompanied to any appreciable extent by increase in the percentage of twins, although it was an advantage in those cases in which twins were born. Similarly, Pearl has shown that there is no significant correlation between the number of mammæ of a sow and the size of her litter.

The effects of inbreeding and crossbreeding on fertility are discussed later. For the present it will suffice to say that inbreeding is very likely to lead to a reduction of fertility, both as regards regularity of breeding and number at a birth. That this is an inevitable result is not, however, indicated by experiment. Among a number of inbred lines, some will be found which appear to suffer little or no loss of fertility. Experiments indicate that the fertility of a herd which has declined through inbreeding can usually be restored by an outcross even with another inbred line of reduced fertility, if the latter is not closely related.

Among factors other than heredity, a warm climate, a reasonable amount of exercise, and a condition neither fat nor thin are conducive to fertility in both males and females. Insufficient exercise is considered to be an especially common cause of failure of stallions. Undernourishment reduces the activity of the reproductive function in both males and females. Excessive fatness is, however, as great a cause of failure to breed in both sexes, in some cases owing to mechanical closure of ducts, in others to fatty degeneration of the sex glands, leading to permanent sterility. Sterility from this cause is a recognized danger in fitting breeding stock for the show ring.

A gaining condition at the time of conception, following a somewhat thin condition, is considered most conducive to fertility. This principle is much used in Great Britain in the so-called practice of flushing ewes. Ewes which have been maintained on pasture are fed liberally for about 3 weeks before breeding, using, especially, succulent feeds. Similarly, fresh, green pasture is recommended for cows which have failed to breed. On the other hand, certain feeds, among which sugar and molasses may be mentioned, are considered likely to lead to sterility.

There are a considerable number of pathological causes of infertility. By far the most important is the financial loss which it occasions is contagious abortion of cattle, a germ disease. Other causes of abortion are also sources of much loss. A small percentage of animals are congenitally sterile. The freemartin heifer is an example which is discussed later. Permanent sterility which is not congenital may result from fatty degeneration, as already mentioned, or from tumors. There are, finally, a number of conditions causing sterility, some of which can be overcome by the use of artificial insemination. The subject is too large to be more than touched on here.

HYBRIDS.

While wide crosses within the same species tend to increase fertility, crosses between different species are apt to result in offspring which are either wholly sterile or of reduced fertility in the few cases in which such crosses can be made at all. The rather common stories of crosses between the sheep and hog may be stated confidently to have no foundation. It is even doubtful whether hybrids can be produced from two such closely related animals as the sheep and the goat, or the dog and the fox. A few possibly authentic instances have been reported, but at best a successful cross appears to be exceedingly unusual in both these cases. The European breeds of cattle cross freely with the Indian humped cattle, although the latter are considered to be of a different species. The cross with the American bison has often been made, the progeny being called cataloes. Some of the females are fertile, but the few males born alive have been sterile. Fertile males have been obtained by backcrossing with the parental species.

The most important species cross among mammals is, of course, that of the horse and ass. Both sexes of the mule, produced by a jack and a mare, and of the hinny, produced by a stallion and a jennet, are probably always sterile. There are occasional reports of fertile mare mules, but none of these seem to have been established beyond doubt. Both the horse and ass will cross with the various species of zebra, producing hybrids which so far as known are always sterile. A number of sterile hybrids have been produced in crosses between the domestic fowl, guinea fowl, peacock, pheasant, etc.

THE REPRODUCTIVE CELLS IN RELATION TO HEREDITY.

GENERAL CONSIDERATIONS.

As already noted, every individual begins his career in the union of two reproductive cells. All that is inherited from his ancestors is somehow passed on by these microscopic bits of living jelly. Any attempt to understand heredity should thus begin with a consideration of these cells and their mode of production by the parents.

At one time it was supposed that the reproductive cells were produced in some way by contributions from all parts of the body, building up, as it were, a miniature organism, ready to develop into an adult under the proper conditions. The egg and sperm cells were thus supposed to transmit the characteristics of the parents as they were at the time of their production. It was taken for granted that the powers of hereditary transmission of an individual could be changed by training, care, or even accident in such way that his subsequent offspring would show a special tendency to develop the new characteristics.

This view was first seriously questioned when it was found that the reproductive cells, like all other cells in the body, are produced only by the division of previous cells. Certain cells remain unspecialized from the beginning of development and after repeated divisions produce the reproductive cells and these only. The remaining cells undergo specialization into skin, muscle, bone, nerve cells, etc., and never give rise to reproductive cells. The two classes of cells, reproductive cells and body cells, thus have separate histories, and any influence of one group on the other must be indirect.

It will easily be seen that this leads to a very different conception of heredity from that mentioned above. The reproductive cells are not produced by the body. They are simply an unchanged bit of the same material which previously developed into the body of the parent. Heredity consists merely in their retention of the power to develop into a complete individual under the proper conditions. Thus, so far as heredity is concerned, the way in which an individual is related to his parents and more remote ancestors does not differ essentially from the kind of relationship with brothers, uncles, etc.

This view of heredity was first reached by Sir Francis Galton, in England, and August Weismann, in Germany, from a consideration of the history of the reproductive cells. Numerous experiments have also been made to test its truth. A striking illustration is given by an experiment performed by Prof. W. E. Castle and Dr. John C. Phillips, of Harvard University. They removed the ovaries of a female albino guinea pig and placed in her body the ovaries of an immature black female, aged about 3 weeks. The albino female was later mated with an albino male. Albinos, mated together, never produce any but albino young, a fact well known to all breeders of small mammals. Yet in this case, the young, six in number, were all black. These young were in three litters, born from 6 months to a year after the operation. The immature ovaries of the black female were subject to the influence of the blood of the albino for from 4 to 10 months before the egg cells attained full growth and were discharged. Through it all they retained their original hereditary potentialities unchanged.

MODIFICATION OF HEREDITY.

Although the reproductive cells are not produced by the body, the possibility must be recognized that they may be modified in some cases by substances circulating in the blood. Recent experiments have, in fact, shown that changes can be brought about in the general vigor of the offspring in this way. Dr. C. R. Stockard, of Cornell University, tested the effect of daily intoxication of guinea pigs with alcohol. The animals themselves remained vigorous throughout the treatment. Their young, however, were markedly unthrifty compared with those of an unintoxicated control stock. This was true even when an alcoholic male was mated with a normal female, indicating that the reproductive cells of the male had been damaged by the alcohol. The injury seemed to be permanent, since a second generation produced by first generation animals, which had never been treated, was likewise feeble. Prof. L. J. Cole, of the University of Wisconsin, has obtained similar results on treating male rabbits with lead. Several other experiments have been made along this general line, some of which confirm the preceding results, while others were negative. It seems clear that it is possible to injure the hereditary qualities of the reproductive cells by means of substances in the blood, but that it is not at all easy to do so.

INHERITANCE OF ACQUIRED CHARACTERISTICS.

The question whether a specific change in the sire, due to training, care, or accident, can be transmitted to the young, is quite independent of the question whether a general loss of vigor can be produced in any such way. As we have seen, the latter can be accomplished through the use of poisons, such as alcohol or lead, and the possibility exists that extreme malnutrition may sometimes have such an effect. The mechanism is at least easy to understand. This is not the case with a specific characteristic.

There is a strong negative evidence in certain cases. Weismann cut off the tails of mice for 19 generations without causing any modification of the young. Docking the tail of sheep and many similar practices have no hereditary effect. Thus it can be stated very positively that the effects of mutilation or accidental injuries are not inherited.

With regard to the functional characteristics in which livestock breeders are most interested, the evidence is not so clear cut but is still negative when of a critical character. F. R. Marshall has shown that the average age of the sires of 2.10 trotters was practically the same as that for all Standardbred horses of the same period, indicating that longer training has no effect on the speed of the progeny. F. S. Putney made an analysis of the records of the Jersey herd at the Missouri Agricultural College and found no relation between age of dam and butterfat record of the daughter.

The failure of acquired characteristics to be inherited does not mean, of course, that proper care and feeding of livestock can be neglected, even from the standpoint of breeding. It is only by testing the speed of his race horses, the butterfat record of his dairy cows, or the fattening capacity of meat animals that the breeder can determine which are likely to transmit the best heredity and so separate the desirable breeding stock from the culls. Moreover, in such a case as the development of an unsoundness in a horse, due apparently to an accident, there should be much hesitation before breeding. The development of the unsoundness is likely to indicate a hereditary weakness, and such horses will be found in general to have sired unsatisfactory colts before the accident and will continue to do so thereafter.

Thus in many respects the breeder should act much as if acquired characteristics were inherited. On the other hand, it is important to know that it is hopeless to attempt to improve scrub stock merely by giving it the best of care for any number of generations.

Probably the strongest reason for the common belief in the inheritance of acquired characteristics is that to many it seems impossible to account for progress in any other way. To this it may be said that while the hereditary qualities of the reproductive cells do not seem to be influenced by changes in the individual, they are not unchangeable. Variations occur from time to time, apparently at random. By the methods discussed later these variations may be combined in desirable ways and fixed in a stock.

TELEGONY.

It was widely believed at one time that after a female has borne young, sired by a certain male, her later offspring, sired by other males, will show characteristics derived from the first—a supposed phenomenon which has been called telegony. Such an influence could come only from a modification of the egg cells of the female by influences from the first offspring before birth, and so come under the head of the inheritance of acquired characteristics. It is even more improbable, however, as the influence of the first male must necessarily be very indirect. The most widely quoted example of this sort of influence was a case in which a mare was mated with a zebra, producing a hybrid, and later, after mating with a horse, produced a colt which had certain markings which resembled those of a zebra. This, however, was merely an isolated case. A considerable number of attempts have been made to confirm it, but with no success. The most extensive experiments were those of J. Cossar Ewart, likewise with zebras and mares. He could find no effects which could be ascribed to telegony. There was, indeed, one case in which a mare produced a colt with vestiges of stripes after having produced a hybrid. It was found, however, that the sire of this colt, an Arab, produced similarly striped colts from mares which had never seen a zebra.

Similar experiments with zebra crosses, also with negative results, have been carried on by the Bureau of Animal Industry. F. B. Mumford and C. B. Hutchinson made an investigation of the question in the mule-breeding district of Missouri. Many cases were found in which mares bore mule and horse colts successively, but no evidence could be found for telegony. The theory is now considered to be thoroughly discredited and is evidently one which need give the practical breeder no concern.

MATERNAL IMPRESSIONS.

There is another very ancient belief which may be mentioned in this connection. This is the belief that objects seen by a prospective mother, especially if a nervous shock is produced, have an effect on the unborn young. Such an influence appears highly improbable in the light of our present knowledge, as there is no nervous connection between mother and offspring or even a direct blood connection. The favorable evidence is all of the unsatisfactory character of anecdotes, while deliberate attempts to obtain the phenomenon have all failed. The kind of case which was formerly often explained in this way, such as the appearance of a red calf in a black Aberdeen Angus herd, is now accounted for in other ways.

DETAILS OF HEREDITARY TRANSMISSION.

BLENDING AND ALTERNATIVE INHERITANCE.

Until rather recently it was usual to consider the contributions of the two parents to the heredity of the offspring to be as inseparably mixed together as would be two liquids. This view is illustrated in the common figure of speech used in referring to the degree of heredity from a given stock. Thus the cross between a Merino and a Shropshire sheep is spoken of as half-blood Merino and half-blood Shropshire and is expected to show a blending of the two breeds in all their characteristics. Another Shropshire cross produces a three-quarter blood, which is expected to be intermediate in all respects between the half-blood and the full-blood Shropshire.

This simple formula is still as good as any in predicting the results of a cross about which nothing is known but the characteristics of the two animals which are mated, and even in a large class of cases in which a great deal more is known.

Certain cases, however, have long been known in which this fusion of characteristics does not take place. This is especially likely to be true of coat colors. Every one knows, for example, that a great variety of sharply distinct colors—black, maltese, tabby, orange, etc.—may be found within a single litter of kittens.

The gap between sharply alternative inheritance of this kind and apparent blending inheritance is bridged over by the large class of cases in which the first generation of a cross is more or less of a blend, but the second generation shows greatly increased variability, the different characteristics of the two races tending to reappear in all combinations.

HEREDITARY UNITS.

The basis for any kind of inheritance, of course, must be material contributed by the microscopic sperm and egg cells in their union. The fundamental conception of the present theory of heredity is that these contributions are composed of units which are handed on generation after generation without change. The union of sperm cell and ovum in its bearing on heredity may be compared to the mingling of two collections of solid beads instead of to a mixing of two liquids. Certain characteristics, such as coat color, depend on such a small number of these units for their development that the separate ones can easily be identified, given symbols, and followed from generation to generation. Most characteristics, including size and conformation, depend on such a large number of units for development that the effects of the separate ones can not easily be distinguished. The inheritance is naturally more or less of the blending type, but a large number of phenomena, such as prepotency and the effects of inbreeding and crossbreeding, can be understood best by the theory that the hereditary basis is composed of a limited though fairly large number of unchanging units.

The statement that these units are unchanging applies to ordinary experience. It must not be taken too literally, however, as if this were true there could be no progress. Cases have been clearly established in which a unit must have become modified so that its effect is changed or, in many cases, apparently wholly lost. Differences between individuals depend on the possession of different alternative forms of certain of the hereditary units.

It may be added that the experimental evidence indicates that there is in general equal inheritance from sire and dam with respect to all kinds of characters. With the exception of a rather unusual class of cases, which is discussed later, it appears that the sperm cell contains a full set of the hereditary units characteristic of the kind of animal and that the same is true of the egg cell. The fertilized egg cell thus receives a double set of the units.

COLOR AND ALBINISM IN GUINEA PIGS.

A concrete illustration will bring out the behavior of these hereditary units in a typical case. It has been mentioned already that albino guinea pigs always breed true. Stocks of colored guinea pigs can also be obtained which breed true in the sense that they never produce albinos. The first cross between such stocks results wholly in colored young. Color, therefore, is said to dominate over albinism, and, conversely, albinism is said to be recessive to color. If these crossbred young, whether male or female, are bred back to the albino stock, it will be found that only 50 per cent of the young are colored, the other half being albinos. These albinos, when crossed with each other, produce only albinos, and this is true of their descendants indefinitely. The power to produce color seems to have completely dropped out of their make-up. If their colored brothers or sisters are crossed with the albino stock, the result is, as before, 50 per cent colored to 50 per cent albino. These last colored young are seven-eighths blood of the albino stock, yet when crossed with albinos they again produce 50 per cent colored and 50 per cent albino. No matter how many albino top crosses are made, the colored animals continue to produce colored young in numbers which never depart to a significant extent from 50 per cent.

The animals of the original stock are supposed to have a certain hereditary unit in their make-up which we may call factor C, following the custom of representing a dominant unit by a capital letter. The albino stock have a modification of this factor, c, which is no longer able to play its normal part in the production of color. All

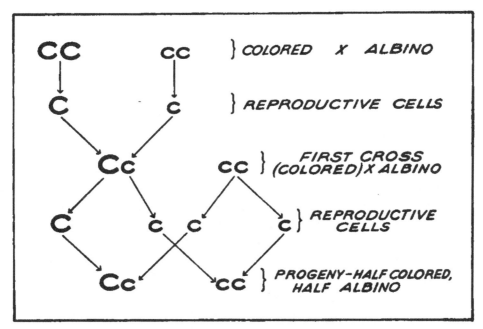

Fig. 2.—Diagram illustrating the mode of inheritance of a unit Mendelian factor. A pure colored strain of guinea pig (CC) is crossed with albinos (cc). Their progeny are all colored (Cc), but produce two kinds of reproductive cells, one transmitting color (C) and other albinism (c), as is revealed by a cross with albino stock.

the reproductive cells of the colored stock have factor C, those of the albino stock factor c. On crossing the two stocks, a fertilized egg cell is produced which must possess both. The evidence indicates, however, that the two units remain side by side in the cell, without the slightest influence on each other, and in each cell division, as the animal develops, each unit divides, with the result that every cell in the body is similar to the fertilized egg in containing both C and c. In the appropriate parts of the body—skin, eyes, and hair—factor C cooperates with other factors in the production of color, and, as a single unit appears to be sufficient in this case, the crossbred guinea pigs (Cc) are as strongly colored as the original colored stock in which factor C is received by each pig from both eggs and sperm (CC).

In the formation of the reproductive cells, it must be assumed that the double set of units is sorted into two single sets. The crossbred colored guinea pigs (Cc) produce two kinds of reproductive cells in equal numbers, those transmitting color (C) and those transmitting albinism (c). On crossing with an albino it is obvious that two classes of the young will be produced in equal numbers, depending on whether the reproductive cells of the latter (c) happen to unite with a cell transmitting color (C) or one transmitting albinism (c). The albino young (cc) have no more tendency to transmit color than pure albino stock, while the colored young (Cc), although three-quarter blood albino, are of the same hereditary make-up as the first cross and so breed like them.

MENDELIAN INHERITANCE.

This mode of inheritance was first worked out about half a century ago by an Austrian monk, Gregor Johann Mendel, who experimented with a number of alternative characteristics of the garden pea. The same principles have been found to apply to an enormous number of characteristics in both plants and animals and are now believed to be true of all heredity. Most cases appear more complicated than the case of the colored and white guinea pigs, because most characteristics depend on the cooperation of a large number of independently inherited unit factors. Occasionally there is also the complication that the same unit may have an influence on the development of a number of seemingly independent characteristics.

There are a number of technical terms which ordinarily are used in discussion of heredity which it will be well to mention. Unit factors which are alternatives of each other in inheritance, one presumably being a modification of the other, are called allelomorphs of each other. Thus factors C and c are allelomorphs. Two other modifications or allelomorphs of factor C are known, which determine degrees of intensity of color intermediate between full intensity and the white of albinos (c^d and c^r). Animals produced by the union of an egg and a sperm which contain the same unit in a given set of allelomorphs are said to be homozygous in that particular. Guinea pigs of the formulas CC, $c^d c^d$, $c^r c^r$, and cc are all homozygous. Each produces only one kind of reproductive cell so far as this set of factors is concerned. Where the alternative factors are different, the animal is said to be heterozygous. Guinea pigs of the formulas Cc^d, Cc^r, Cc, $c^d c^r$, $c^d c^a$, and $c^r c^a$ are all heterozygous. Each produces two kinds of reproductive cells in equal numbers. It is impossible for a guinea pig to transmit more than two of the grades of intensity, a conclusion which has been very thoroughly established by experiments.

Factor C has been spoken of as producing colored young, but no particular color was mentioned. This is because it alone does not determine any particular color. It merely cooperates with other factors. One of the other factors, which we may represent by the symbol E, enables black pigment to develop. Its alternative, e, permits only red to develop. The first cross between a black stock ($CCEE$) and a red stock ($CCee$) is black ($CCEe$). Thus black is dominant over red. The first-cross animals produce reproductive cells containing E and e, respectively, in equal numbers. Since factor E and its allelomorph e are wholly independent of factor C and its allelomorphs, it is possible for a guinea pig to have any combination of the two sets. Thus an albino may transmit black only ($ccEE$) or red only ($ccee$) or both ($ccEe$). Suppose that an albino

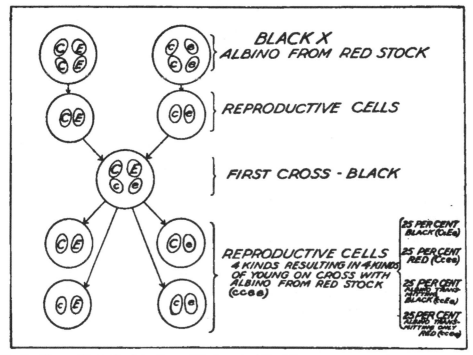

FIG. 3.—Diagram illustrating inheritance of 2 independent Mendelian factors. A pure-black strain of guinea pig ($CCEE$) is crossed with albinos from red stock ($ccee$). The young of the first cross are all black but produce four kinds of reproductive cells in equal numbers, as revealed by appropriate crosses.

of the second type ($ccee$) is crossed with a black stock which breeds true ($CCEE$); the first cross will be colored (Cc) and the color will be black (Ee). If, now, these crossbred blacks are bred with the same albino stock, we expect half the young to be colored (Cc) and half to be albino (cc). Of the colored young, half should be black ($CcEe$) and half red ($Ccee$). The albinos will be divided similarly into two classes, those which transmit black in half their reproductive cells ($ccEe$) and those which transmit only red ($ccee$). These two classes, however, will look alike. The cross thus should produce 50 per cent albinos, 25 per cent reds, and 25 per cent blacks, which it actually does.

Without going into more detail it may be said that six independent sets of allelomorphs are known in guinea pigs which cooperate to determine color. The combinations of these factors determine over a hundred distinguishable colors.

THE CHROMOSOMES AND HEREDITY.

The present theory of heredity was devised to explain the results of experiments such as those given above. Recent studies of cells under the microscope have apparently brought the mechanism under our eyes. It has already been mentioned that proper methods of staining bring out a certain definite number of rod-shaped bodies, the chromosomes, in the cells of each kind of animal or plant. The reproductive cells are found to contain just half as many as the fertilized egg and the body cells. At each ordinary cell division the chromosomes arrange themselves in a ring, each splits lengthwise, and half goes to one daughter cell, half to the other. Thus all the body cells have a double set. In the formation of the reproductive cells, on the other hand, the chromosomes do not split, but the homologous ones, derived from the sperm and egg, pair with each other and then separate, one going to each daughter cell. The reproductive cells thus get only a single set of chromosomes. It will easily be seen that if the hereditary units were located in the chromosomes the observed behavior of the latter would fully account for the laws of heredity illustrated above.

Summing up, genetic experiments prove the double nature of individuals and the single nature of their reproductive cells in regard to each set of alternative hereditary factors, while the microscope actually shows us the chromosomes in pairs in the body cells in place of the single set to be observed in the reproductive cells.

LINKAGE.

As the study of heredity has advanced, a number of complications have been found. These complications, however, have only made closer the parallelism between the facts of heredity and the observed behavior of the chromosomes. The most important of these complications is the phenomenon known as linkage. A case studied by Prof. Castle and the writer will serve as an example.

A few years ago a freak wild rat with yellow fur and red eyes was trapped on a wharf in England. Another wild rat of the same color, but with pink eyes, was trapped in another place. Two strains of yellow rats were developed which could be distinguished only by the color of the eyes. Each strain bred true. Crosses with normal wild rats showed that only one recessive unit factor was involved in each case. It may appear surprising that on crossing the two yellow strains with each other, all the young looked practically like ordinary gray rats with black eyes. This result was not, however, wholly unexpected. It is rather common to find that two variations which look alike are due to different factors, so that, on crossing, each supplies the normal factor lacking in the other, and the young appear to be normal. If we represent the wild gray rats by formula *PPRR*, the red-eyed yellows by *PPrr*, and the pink-eyed yellows by *ppRR*, we indicate that each kind of yellow is recessive and breeds true by itself, but on intercrossing produces a variety *PpRr*, which contains both of the dominant normal factors, and thus appears like a wild gray.

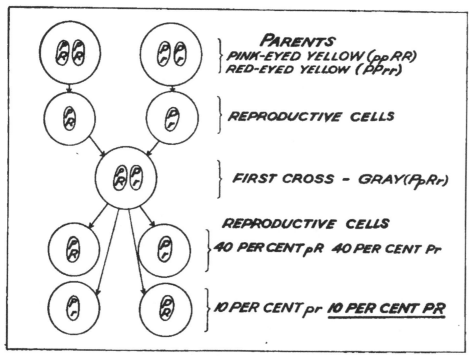

Fig. 4.—Diagram illustrating linkage. The pink-eyed and the red-eyed strains of yellow rats depend on different recessive factors. As each supplies the normal factor lacking in the other, crossing results in normal black-eyed grays. These grays produce reproductive cells in which the factors tend to be associated in the same combination as that in which they entered the cross, due, it is believed, to their transmission in the same chromosome. Only about 10 per cent of the reproductive cells are found to transmit both normal factors (*PR*).

On raising a second generation, a few pink-eyed yellows were found, which proved to transmit the red-eyed as well as the pink-eyed variation in all of their reproductive cells. Their formula would be *pprr*. On crossing this strain with ordinary wild rats (*PPRR*), we obtain gray young, which should have the same formula (*PpRr*) as the first cross between the two strains of yellows. The two kinds of first-cross grays were backcrossed with the above-mentioned double recessive pink-eyed yellow strain (*pprr*) by Prof. Castle in order to test the formulæ.

This would seem to be the same kind of cross as that discussed previously, in which black guinea pigs transmitting both red and albinism (*CcEe*) were crossed with albinos of red stock (*ccee*). We should expect half the reproductive cells of the crossbreds to contain factor *P*, and half of these should also contain factor *R*. Thus, one-quarter of the young should receive both normal factors from the crossbred gray parent and be gray themselves. This, however, was not the result. When grays derived from the cross between the original two strains of yellows (*PPrr* and *ppRR*) were used, only 174 out of 1,714 young were gray, about 10 per cent. When the gray parent came from the cross between wild grays (*PPRR*) and

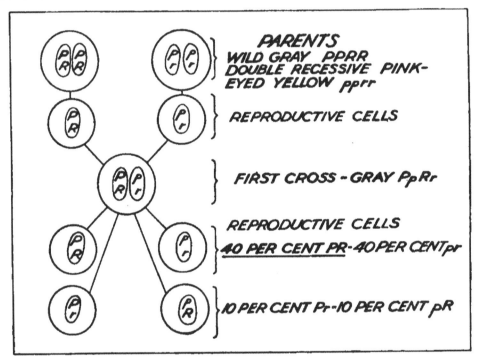

FIG. 5.—Diagram illustrating linkage. The cross between wild gray rats and double recessive pink-eyed yellows results in gray young with the same formula as in the cross between the two yellow strains. They breed differently, however, since in this case the two normal factors enter the cross together, instead of apart. About 40 per cent of their reproductive cells are found to transmit both normal factors in this case instead of 10 per cent.

the double recessive pink-eyed yellows (*pprr*), 1,255 out of 3,032 young were gray, or more than 40 per cent. In the second case there is as much excess over the expected 25 per cent as there was defect in the first case. The explanation is that the two sets of factors *P, p* and *R, r* are not wholly independent of each other in heredity. An individual produced, as in the second case, by the union of reproductive cells *PR* and *pr* tends to produce reproductive cells of these kinds in excess over the kinds *Pr* and *pR*. The situation is reversed in an individual produced, as in the first case, by the union of reproductive cells *Pr* and *pR*. This tendency of certain sets of factors to stick together in the formation of the reproductive cells, according to the way in which they were combined in the production of the individual himself, is known as linkage.

A third color variation in rats, viz, albinism, has been found to be linked with both of the yellow variations. On the other hand, the other known color variations, white spotting and black, are not only inherited wholly independently of each other, but also of albinism and the two kinds of yellows.

This phenomenon of linkage has been found to be very widespread. The first case was found by Professors Bateson and Punnett, of Cambridge University, in the sweet pea. Cases are known in corn and oats, in the primrose and snapdragon, in chickens and pigeons, in mice as well as in rats, in grasshoppers, silkworms, and flies. By far the most thoroughly analyzed case is that of the fruit fly, Drosophila, in which Prof. T. H. Morgan and his coworkers, of Columbia University, have studied hundreds of Mendelian variations. They find that these variations fall into four groups, such that within each group every factor is linked more or less with every other factor, while there is never any linkage between factors in different groups. It is not merely a coincidence that in this fruit fly there are just four pairs of chromosomes.

This statement suggests the accepted explanation of linkage. Factors which are carried by the same chromosome tend to stick together. The chromosomes appear to maintain their identity through all the ordinary cell divisions. Just before the formation of the reproductive cells, the homologous chromosomes come together and twist around each other, giving a chance for an interchange of pieces. The degree of linkage between two factors is believed to measure their distance apart within the chromosome. On this basis Prof. Morgan and his coworkers have actually been able to make maps showing the location of a great number of unit factors in the different chromosomes of the fruit fly, which explain the results of crosses in a very convincing way.

The most remarkable corroboration of the chromosome theory of heredity has been the bringing of the genetic phenomenon of linkage and the visible behavior of the chromosomes into relation with the solution of the ancient problem of sex determination.

THE DETERMINATION OF SEX.

THE NORMAL METHOD.

There are few questions connected with animal breeding which have aroused so much interest from the earliest times as the determination of sex. Hundreds of theories have been advanced, and, though repeatedly disproved, keep reappearing. It is only within the twentieth century that the means by which sex is at least usually determined in the higher animals has been discovered. This mechanism, however, seems to be one that is beyond human interference.

It has been noted that a certain definite number of chromosomes can be seen under the microscope in the cells of each kind of animal. A qualification of this statement, connected with the determina-

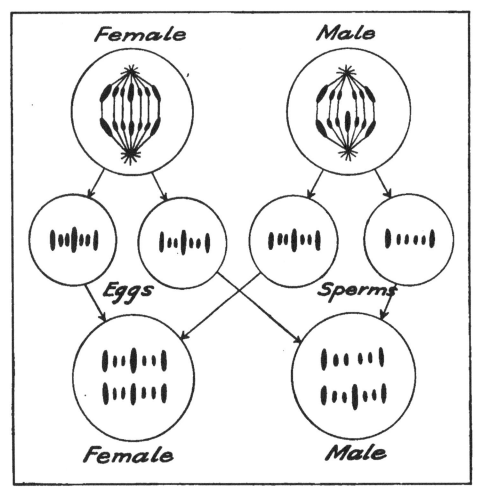

FIG. 6.—Diagram illustrating the method of sex determination in an animal with 14 chromosomes in the cells of the females, 13 in the males. All eggs have 7 chromosomes but only half the sperms have 7 chromosomes, the other half having 6. The former are female-determining sperms, the latter male determiners. Hereditary factors carried by the sex-determining chromosomes pass with it from father to daughter, never from father to son in such cases as that illustrated above.

tion of sex, was suggested in 1902 by Prof. C. E. McClung, on the basis of a study of the cells of grasshoppers. This suggestion has since been confirmed in principle by a large number of scientists working with widely different kinds of animals, ranging from worms to mammals. In most cases that have been studied carefully a difference has been found between the sexes, either in the number of the chromosomes or in the size of one pair.

As an illustration, we will consider the case of one of the grasshoppers in which, owing to the large size of the cells and the relatively small number of chromosomes, the facts are considered to be beyond question. In this case, study of the cells from the digestive tract and muscle fibers of males shows 6 pairs of similar chromosomes and 1 odd chromosome, making 13 in all. The body cells of females contain 7 pairs of chromosomes, 6 pairs of which resemble the pairs in the male, while those in the seventh pair resemble the odd chromosome of the male. The same numbers are found in the reproductive cells before the final division which results in the functional reproductive cells. The final division is peculiar, as already noted, in that the chromosomes are sorted bodily into two groups. All the egg cells must contain 7 chromosomes, 1 from each pair. The sperm cells, on the other hand, are necessarily of two kinds, half containing 6 and half 7. The two kinds must, of course, be formed in exactly equal numbers. The inference is clear that any egg cell which happens to be fertilized by a sperm containing 6 chromosomes will develop into a grasshopper with only 13 chromosomes in the body cells, and hence a male, while fertilization by a sperm containing the odd chromosome, i. e., 7 chromosomes in all, will result in the number 14, and hence a female. From this it appears that sex is determined by chance at the moment of fertilization.

A similar mechanism has been found in a number of the mammals, including man. In the latter case, according to Von Winiwarter, there are 23 chromosomes in the male-determining sperms and 24 in those which determine the female sex.

It is naturally more difficult to establish the facts beyond question where such large numbers are involved. Fortunately, however, there is a wholly independent line of evidence which leads to the same conclusion. This is the evidence from characteristics linked with sex in inheritance.

SEX-LINKED INHERITANCE.

In the human species the mode of inheritance is best understood in the case of abnormalities which keep appearing in particular families. Most of these traits are inherited as if due to a single dominant or recessive factor. There are a number, however, including color blindness and hemophilia, which have long been known to follow a very peculiar mode of inheritance. These traits usually affect only males, yet are never transmitted from father to son, and do not reappear in the descendants of the sons. The daughters of affected males, on the other hand, though not affected themselves, are very apt to have affected sons. This rule was discovered as early as 1820 by Nasse in the case of hemophilia, a condition in which the blood fails to clot properly, with the consequence that an affected individual may bleed to death from a slight scratch.

Until recently the explanation of this kind of inheritance was a complete mystery. A little consideration, however, will show that it is exactly what should be expected of a trait due to a factor carried by the chromosome which determines sex. The evidence indicates that in the human species this so-called X chromosome is single in males and paired in females. Half of the sperm cells produced by a male contain the X chromosome and hence can transmit hereditary traits which it contains. These are the female-determining sperms. The other half, the male-determiners, lack the X chromosome and all that is transmitted by it. This explains why a sex-linked characteristic can not be transmitted from father to son or to any of the descendants of the latter. All the daughters of an affected male receive the abnormal factor in the X chromosome which determines their sex. They will not, however, show the abnormality themselves, if it is recessive, as they also in general receive a normal X chromosome from their mother. Half of their ova, however, will contain the affected X chromosome. Those fertilized by sperms which lack the X chromosome are sons, and they will show the abnormality, as they can receive no protecting normal factor from the father.

The common yellow variation of cats is another example of a characteristic which is linked with sex in this way, except for the fact that dominance is lacking. We may represent an X chromosome containing the factor for yellow by X_y, and one containing the alternative factor for black by X_b. There are three kinds of female cats in this respect, yellow ($X_y X_y$), tortoise-shell ($X_y X_b$), and black ($X_b X_b$). Males, however, having only one X chromosome, can be of only two kinds, yellow (X_y—) and black (X_b—). It has, in fact, long been known that tortoise-shell males are so rare as to be classed as freaks. It should be added that there are independent factors which may change black in either sex to maltese or the tabby pattern.

The female-determining sperm cells contain the extra chromosome (X_y in the case of a yellow male, X_b in the case of a black male). The male-determining sperm cells wholly lack this chromosome. Thus a male can have no influence on the color of his sons so far as this pair of factors in concerned. A black female produces only black sons, a yellow female produces only yellow sons, and a tortoise-shell female produces 50 per cent of each on the average regardless of the color of the male in each case. A male can, however, transmit his color to the sons of his daughters.

In an earlier section it was noted that Prof. Morgan and his co-workers had found that the hereditary variations of the fruit fly fall into four linkage groups, corresponding to the four pairs of chromosomes of this insect. Microscopical study shows that sex is determined by one of these chromosomes in essentially the same way as that found in the grasshoppers and mammals in that the male produces two kinds of sperm. Parallel to this, they find that all the factors in one of the four linkage groups follow the sex-linked mode of inheritance of hemophilia and color blindness in man and the yellow color in cats.

A number of characteristics have been found in chickens, pigeons, and canaries which are linked with sex, but curiously enough the relation to sex is exactly the reverse of that described above. The barred pattern of Plymouth Rock fowls is a familiar example. When a barred male is mated with a black female all the chicks are barred. With a black male and a barred female, only the male chicks are barred, the females being black. Further tests show that the barred females in the first case have no more tendency to transmit black than pure-blood Plymouth Rocks, while in the second case the black females have no tendency to transmit barring. There is, in other words, no inheritance of either of the alternative characters from mother to daughter. The conclusion drawn from such experiments is that in birds the females produce two kinds of eggs—determining the male and female sexes, respectively—while the males produce only one kind of sperm. Prof. Raymond Pearl, of the Maine experiment station, found indications that the difference in fecundity between Plymouth Rocks and Cornish Indian Games was in part inherited in this way.

This method of sex determination is not limited to birds. It was found in a moth by Prof. Doncaster, of Cambridge University, in the first case of sex-linked inheritance to be analyzed, and has been demonstrated in the silkworm by Toyoma and Tanaka, two Japanese scientists.

THE SEX RATIO.

According to the method of determination outlined above, the sexes should be produced in equal numbers in the long run. This, in fact, is very nearly true in all the higher animals. Nevertheless, it is undoubtedly true that there is generally not exact equality. An extensive investigation in Germany by M. Wilckens gave the following numbers of males born to every 100 females: Cattle, 107.3; horses, 97.3; sheep, 97.4; swine, 111.8. The sex ratio in man varies in different countries, but always shows an excess of males, the average ratio being about 105 males to 100 females. These deviations of the sex ratio from equality are not necessarily out of harmony with the present theory of sex determination. The two kinds of sperm cells, for example, may differ in their activity or vitality.

Thus, while it appears very doubtful whether sex can ever be controlled in any exact way, the possibility of varying the sex ratio must be recognized. The results of even this very limited degree of control of sex determination, however, have been disappointing to date. Slight differences in the sex ratio among young born in different times of the year have often been published, but the results are so inconsistent that no general conclusion can be drawn. Another common theory is that a better nutritive condition of the dam favors the production of females. Great quantities of statistics have been gathered on this subject, but the evidence indicates an excess of males as often as of females under favorable conditions. Again it is believed by some that the sex of the more vigorous parent preponderates among the young, and by others the reverse is held. The two antagonistic theories seem to have just as much and as little support. The same is true of the theories which connect the relative or absolute ages of the parents with the sex of the offspring. A belief which is especially common among cattle breeders is that the time of services after the beginning of heat determines sex. The most common form of the theory is that early service tends to result in a preponderance of females, while service late in heat means more males. This theory has been most thoroughly tested by Prof. Pearl in data obtained from Maine farmers. His earlier data seemed to support the theory, but after adequate numbers had been obtained no significant differences remained.

The view that sex, or at least sex ratio, can be modified by control of such factors as those listed above has been urged most forcefully in recent years by Dr. Oscar Riddle on the basis of experiments begun by Professor C. O. Whitman with various wild species of pigeons and doves. In these experiments Whitman and Riddle found an excess of males under conditions tending toward heightened vigor and of females under the reverse conditions. In tame pigeons, Cole and Kirkpatrick have shown that the sexes of squabs of the same clutch are distributed wholly at random, indicating the lack of any external control over sex. The departures from a random distribution found by Whitman and Riddle were not very great and their significance still seems to be an open question.

A theory of sex determination which deserves mention only because of the frequency with which it is advanced is that sperm cells from one testicle produce males, from the other females. An alternative theory has it that it is one ovary which produces males, the other females. These theories are very easy to test by experiments in which one testicle or ovary is removed. Such experiments have been performed on a large scale with hogs and rats without any effect on the sex ratio.

The common belief that particular animals have a tendency to produce an excess of males or females has rather more support than the other theories mentioned above. Breeders of dairy cattle in particular often become discouraged with a bull which seems to sire largely bull calves. It must be remembered in this connection, however, that rather large departures from equality may occur simply by chance. Thus if a coin is tossed 20 times, the best expectation is 10 heads and 10 tails, but about once in 40 times a departure as great or greater than 15 heads or tails is to be looked for. Thus a large number of dairy-cattle breeders may be expected to get 15 or more bull calves out of 20 calves born. Such a result in one year would not have the slightest effect on the sex ratio in the next.

However, very extensive experiments with rats, made by Dr. Helen D. King, of the Wistar Institute, have shown that it is possible by selection, accompanied by inbreeding, to produce strains which differ considerably in sex ratio. She obtained 122 males to 100 females in the strain selected for male production and 82 males to 100 females in the strain selected in the opposite direction.

The theory that sex is normally determined by the number of chromosomes brought together by the sperm and egg at fertilization does not necessarily mean that this is the only method. There is, in fact, a certain amount of evidence which indicates that under extreme conditions the sex, as determined by the chromosomes, may be reversed. In hybridizing, especially, the normal mechanism seems likely to be upset and a great excess of males or females may be produced.

THE FREEMARTIN.

An interesting case of incomplete reversal of sex has recently been solved and may be mentioned in this connection. It has long been known that a heifer calf, born as a twin with a bull, is, in 8 or 9 cases out of 10, sterile. Such a heifer is called a "freemartin." The cause of this phenomenon has recently been worked out independently by Tandler and Keller in Germany and by Prof. F. R. Lillie, of the University of Chicago. They found that the blood systems of cattle twins usually grow together. When both twins were females or both males, no harm resulted. When a female was the twin of a male the development of the former appeared wholly normal in the few cases in which the blood systems remained separate. In all the cases in which the blood systems were connected, the female showed an abnormal development, intermediate between that of a female and a male. It appeared that the male embryo secreted some substance into the blood which tended to reverse the sexual development of the female embryo.

MENDELIAN HEREDITY IN LIVESTOCK.

POLLED CATTLE.

We know much less about the details of heredity in the larger animals than in a number of small ones, such as the guinea pig, rabbit, rat, mouse, and especially Prof. Morgan's fruit fly. Nevertheless unit factors have been demonstrated in a considerable number of cases. Polled and horned cattle, for example, differ by a single unit in their heredity. The factor which determines the polled condition is nearly fully dominant over its alternative in horned cattle. In a cross between the polled Aberdeen Angus and the Shorthorn, most of the calves are wholly polled, and the rest, as a rule, merely have loose scurs in the skin. These scurs are more frequent in males than females. The same factor has appeared within the Shorthorn, Hereford, and other breeds and has permitted the formation of polled subbreeds.

Polled bulls produce 100 per cent polled or nearly polled calves if they are homozygous polled like the Aberdeen Angus breed (PP). Otherwise (Pp) they produce 50 per cent polled and 50 per cent horned in crosses with horned cattle (pp). The polled animals can be crossed generation after generation with horned stock without reducing the per cent of polled calves below 50 to a significant extent. Their horned descendants, on the other hand, have no more tendency to transmit the polled condition than ordinary horned cattle. The polled character can easily be fixed if the mode of inheritance is borne in mind in making all matings. The most important point is to use exclusively bulls which have been proved to be homozygous polled (PP). Such bulls can be produced only when both parents are polled. All polled calves produced by a polled bull from a polled cow are not, however, homozygous. Unless it is known that both parents were homozygous, the most promising bull calves among those with scurs small or absent should be picked out and tested with a number of horned cows. It should be easy to find one which transmits only the polled condition.

COLORS OF CATTLE.

The black Aberdeen-Angus, Galloway, and Holstein-Friesian cattle differ in their hereditary make-up from the red breeds (Shorthorn, Hereford, Ayrshire, Devon, etc.) by a unit factor. Black is dominant over red, and thus may transmit it. The red may be handed on for generations out of sight, to appear when two blacks are mated both of which transmit it. Even to-day a red calf occasionally is born in a respectable black herd of Aberdeen-Angus cattle. In such case it is well to remember that the sire, as well as the dam, is transmitting it in half his reproductive cells and had best be replaced.

Another interesting pair of factors is found in the red and white of the Shorthorns. In this case neither is dominant. The heterozygous animals have a mixture of red and white, the familiar roan pattern. The roan is thus an unfixable color. Roan by roan produces only about 50 per cent roan calves, the rest being equally divided between red and white. Practically 100 per cent roan can be obtained by breeding a white bull with red cows, or the reverse. The factor which removes the color from the hair of roans and whites is inherited independently of the kind of color. Thus, when a white Shorthorn bull is bred with black Aberdeen-Angus or Galloway cattle, the black of the latter is dominant over the red factor which is present in white Shorthorns as well as red ones, while the white factor of the Shorthorn is imperfectly dominant over the solid color of the Aberdeen Angus or Galloway. The result is a blue roan. When such blue roans are crossed together, blacks, blue roans, whites with black ears, reds, red roans, and whites with red ears, are all produced if enough calves are born. All but the last class were found among 21 calves produced in such an experiment at the Iowa agricultural experiment station.

Other colors in cattle have not been worked out so satisfactorily. There appears, however, to be an imperfectly dominant dilution factor which reduces black to dun color and red to fawn. The white patterns of many breeds are inherited independently of their colors and are, at least to some extent, dominant. The white face of the Hereford is thus transmitted to nearly all the calves in the first generation of a cross whether the rest of the coat is black or red, and is a useful "trade-mark" for the recognition of Hereford grades in the market. Grades of the dairy breeds are usually recognized by showing traces of the dilute color of Jerseys or Guernseys or the large, irregular, white areas of Ayrshires, Holstein-Friesian, and many Guernseys.

COLORS OF HORSES.

The colors of horses have been worked out in much detail. The power to develop black (factor H) seen in bays, blacks, duns, etc., is dominant over its absence, as seen in chestnuts (factor h). Bays (B) differ from blacks (b) by an independent factor which may or may not be transmitted by chestnuts. The dilute colored duns, creams, and mouse-colored horses differ from bays, chestnuts, and blacks, respectively, by a third dominant factor (factor D and d). Three other independent pairs of factors determine between the roan (R), gray (G), and piebald (S) patterns and their absence (r, g, and s). Since a chestnut horse is recessive in all essential factors ($hhddrrggss$), he or she can produce only one kind of reproductive cell ($hdrgs$), and two chestnuts, whatever their ancestry, can produce only chestnut foals.

It was thus very easy to fix the chestnut color in the Sussex Punch breed, but on the other hand, all other colors are dominant or, as is usually said, prepotent over it. The degree of prepotency depends on the dominant factors which are homozygous. A homozygous gray stallion (GG) will produce nothing but gray colts, however crossed. A heterozygous gray (Gg) will produce 50 per cent gray and 50 per cent not gray in crosses with mares which are not gray.

FIG. 7.—The spotted coat pattern of this scrub stallion is due to a dominant hereditary unit and may be expected to appear in half of his progeny. The curby hocks and other unsoundness are also strongly transmissible.

COLORS OF HOGS.

Curiously enough we know less about the mode of inheritance of colors in hogs than in the larger animals. The results of the first crosses between the various breeds are, however, well known. The white of Yorkshires and Chesters is more or less prepotent over the red of Tamworths and Duroc-Jerseys, and, probably for a wholly different reason, over the black of Hampshires, Berkshires, and Poland Chinas. The black of Hampshires is prepotent over the red of the red breeds. Berkshires and Poland Chinas, on the other hand, when mated with the red breeds, produce pigs with a tortoise-shell mixture of black, red, and often white spots. The white belt of Hampshires, like the white patterns of many other animals, is very irregular in its heredity. It is doubtful whether a given type of belt can ever be completely fixed.

COLORS OF SHEEP.

The color of black sheep is recessive to the ordinary white color. It can thus appear only when transmitted by both ram and ewe. It is well to remember that a single black lamb in a flock indicates that the ram is transmitting the unit for black in half his sperm cells. Half of his daughters may thus be expected to transmit it.

COLORS AND COMB SHAPE OF POULTRY.

The mode of inheritance of the colors of poultry is still far from thoroughly worked out, but a few points may be mentioned. The barred pattern of Plymouth Rocks and several other color patterns are linked with sex in the way which has already been discussed.

FIG. 8.—A daughter of the stallion in figure 7. Note the inheritance of the spotted coat pattern and curby hocks.

The Blue Andalusian has a color which is inherited in a way similar to the roan of Shorthorn cattle. It is a color which can not be fixed. Blue by blue produces only 50 per cent blues, the rest being equally divided between blacks and splashed whites. It is possible, however, to produce 100 per cent blue chicks by crossing the blacks and whites with each other.

The mode of inheritance has been worked out for a number of characteristics of poultry besides color. Thus rose comb is dominant over single comb and behaves as if it differed only in one unit factor. The pea comb of Indian Games and Brahmas is also dominant over single comb but depends on a variation of a different unit factor. The combination of rose and pea comb results in the walnut comb of the Malay breeds.

HEREDITY OF FORM AND FUNCTION IN LIVESTOCK.

RELATIONS OF THEORY TO PRACTICE.

In the preceding sections we have attempted to present a brief outline of the present theory of heredity as it has been developed in the main from experiments with small animals and plants. Illustrations were given which show that these principles apply to farm livestock, at least in the case of coat color and a number of other rather superficial characteristics, such as the presence of horns in cattle and shape of comb in poultry. There is every reason for believing that these principles are of general application, and it is hardly too much to say that the normal method of inheritance is now clearly understood. Unfortunately, however, a thorough understanding does not necessarily mean easy control. The peculiarities of form and function appear to be so complex in their mode of inheritance that an understanding of the fundamental laws of heredity is at present valuable to the stock breeder largely from the light which they throw on such long-known methods of breeding as inbreeding, crossbreeding, selection, etc. In the present section most attention will accordingly be paid to these secondary principles.

EQUALITY OF INHERITANCE FROM THE SEXES.

As already noted, there is, in general, equal inheritance from the sexes with respect to all kinds of characteristics. There is, for example, no scientific foundation for such beliefs as that the dam controls the external form, the sire the constitution of the internal organs, or the reverse. The only known exceptions are the rather small class of sex-linked characteristics, which have already been discussed. For reasons other than heredity, the dam naturally has more influence in the birth weight and some other characteristics of young animals, but these effects seem to be outgrown.

The rule that there is in general equal inheritance from the sexes must not be taken as meaning that the sire or dam may not be prepotent in a particular cross on account of reasons other than sex.

PREPOTENCY.

An ideally prepotent animal is one that impresses his characteristics on all his progeny, however mated. There are many unsound beliefs connected with prepotency. It is often believed that it is a characteristic of an animal as a whole, closely related to vigor. Thus it is often held that a strongly masculine type in a male is an indication of general prepotency. This type is desirable in itself as an indication of vigor, which is of the utmost importance in all breeding, but there is no good evidence that prepotency in any other special characteristic is indicated in this way. The idea of general prepotency has also led to the common belief that proved prepotency in one respect, such as color, indicates prepotency in others. Experiments, however, easily prove the falsity of this claim.

A white-faced red Hereford cow with normal horns produces polled, white-faced, black calves when bred to a polled black Aberdeen-Angus bull. An Aberdeen-Angus cow produces the same kind of calf when bred to a Hereford bull. Evidently prepotency lies neither in the sex, the breed, nor the individual, but in the characteristics, polled head, black color (where there is any color besides white), and white face.

Somewhat similarly, a cross made in either way between an Aberdeen Angus and a white Shorthorn produces polled blue-roan calves. Polled head and black color are prepotent, as before, but prepotency is lacking as regards the third pair of opposed characteristics, the solid color of the Aberdeen Angus and the nearly solid white of the Shorthorn.

It is not the whole story, however, to say that certain characteristics are always prepotent. If in the case above, the polled, blue-roan Shorthorn-Angus crossbreds are bred back to a white Shorthorn, only half the calves will be polled, the rest having good horns, and only half will be black in the colored parts of the coat (that is, they will be blue-roan or white, with black ears), the rest being red roans and whites with red ears. Thus, the characters which were fully prepotent in the purebred cease to be so in the crossbred. The difficulty is that the crossbred produces more than one kind of reproductive cell. In the present case, half of the reproductive cells transmit the polled condition and half transmit horns; half transmit black and half transmit red; half transmit the tendency to develop color in the entire coat, as in the Aberdeen Angus, and half transmit the highly reduced condition of color, as in the white Shorthorn. Moreover, the representatives of the three sets of opposed characters are shuffled up and sorted out into the reproductive cells independently of one another. Some of the reproductive cells transmit the combination polled, solid color and black, others polled, solid color and red, and so on through the eight possible combinations.

In this illustration we have used characteristics which have already been discussed as examples of simple Mendelian heredity. Most characteristics probably depend on a much larger number of hereditary units, but, nevertheless, the nature of prepotency is believed to be essentially the same. So far as there is prepotency, it is a property of characteristics (or really of the hereditary units back of the characteristics), not of individuals, breeds, or sexes, and whatever the characteristic, there can be no prepotency unless the individual produces only one kind of reproductive cell so far as it is concerned.

In technical language, prepotency depends primarily on two things: The factors back of the characteristic must be dominant and each pair of factors must be homozygous. Other considerations, such as the number of factors involved and their linkage relations as well as the system of mating, play a part in determining whether the prepotency of an individual dies with him or is handed on to his descendants. Most of these elements of prepotency are beyond control and can simply be accepted thankfully when they appear. It is possible, however, to bring out such prepotency as is in a stock and preserve prepotency when it has appeared by breeding so as to fix the desired characteristics. Fixation means simply to make all the hereditary factors involved homozygous.

VARIATION.

Before discussing the methods of fixing characters it will be well to go briefly into the causes of variation. In the first place it must be recognized that a great deal of variation is not hereditary. Different characteristics are affected in very different degrees by outside conditions. Hereford cattle produce only white-faced, red calves, whether raised under the best of conditions or under the worst. These same conditions, on the other hand, may make all the difference between well-finished animals which win in the show ring and animals which would appear discreditable even to a scrub herd. The way to eliminate this kind of variation, of course, is to give all the stock uniformly favorable conditions.

Unfortunately there is in many cases variation which is neither hereditary nor due to controllable outside conditions. As already pointed out, there are hereditary differences in the average size of litter produced by different breeds of swine. There are also hereditary differences within the breeds, but their influence is so slight that Poland-China sows born in litters of 13 or more have been found to farrow less than one pig more on the average than sows born in litters of one, two, or three. Outside conditions undoubtedly play a part, but to a very large extent the size of litter produced by a sow seems to be beyond control.

Even variations in coat color, at least with respect to pattern, are not always due to heredity. Spotted guinea pigs vary all the way from nearly solid black to solid white. In a mixed stock it is easy to show that the whiter parents have on the average the whiter offspring, and vice versa, but analysis of the figures in a stock raised by the Bureau of Animal Industry indicated that most of the variation was due to chance irregularities in the course of development, and was thus beyond control.

The importance of such irregularities in development can be measured roughly by the degree of asymmetry found. Thus the patterns of hooded rats and Dutch rabbits are much less likely to be asymmetrical than that of piebald guinea pigs, and it is found that a given pattern can be fixed in them much more perfectly. The white face of Hereford cattle is usually symmetrical and has been fixed to a satisfactory extent. Whether the white belt of Hampshire swine can be so fixed seems more doubtful, owing to its frequent asymmetry.

Occasionally a variation is due to the appearance of a wholly new hereditary characteristic in a stock. The polled variation of cattle has probably appeared in this way a number of times. Such variations, or mutations, as they are called, are, however, very rare.

Most hereditary variation is due simply to recombination of the factors already present in the parent stocks. The blue roans and their varied progeny, derived from crosses between Shorthorn and Aberdeen-Angus cattle, are a good illustration of variation of this sort. It is this form of variation only which can be eliminated by methods of breeding.

FIXATION OF HEREDITY BY SELECTION.

Consistent selection toward the desired type is sometimes all that is necessary to fix a characteristic. Unfortunately, experiments have shown that what appear to be the same characteristics in two animals often depend on wholly different combinations of hereditary factors. A good example has been given in another connection in the case of two strains of light-eyed, yellow rats, each of which bred true by itself, but which produced nothing but black-eyed gray rats when crossed with each other. Thus progress by straight selection may be wholly upset at any time by an unfortunate cross of this kind. The whole breed must be lifted up at once if there is to be success by selection alone. Careful selection with breeding confined within a single herd or a few related herds, on the other hand, only requires that this small group be lifted up at once. Once success has been obtained, such a herd or group of herds becomes a powerful source of breed improvement by supplying prepotent sires. Practical experience agrees with theory in the principle that the only systematic method of fixing heredity, and so bringing out such prepotency as is in a stock, is Bakewell's old method of close breeding accompanied by careful selection.

FIXATION OF HEREDITY BY INBREEDING.

The primary effect of inbreeding is the fixation of hereditary qualities, whether good, bad, or indifferent. In other words, a sufficiently inbred animal produces only one kind of reproductive cell with respect to all hereditary characteristics (with the exception of sex and characters linked with sex in the case of male mammals or female birds). The closer the inbreeding, the more rapid will be this fixation of hereditary characteristics.

The reason why inbreeding fixes characteristics is easy to understand. As an illustration, consider a stock of horses in which blacks, bays, and chestnuts are being produced. Recalling that the dominant factor H is necessary in order that any black be present, that is, that the horse be other than a chestnut, and that the dominant factor B in the presence of H determines the bay pattern we see that the three colors may be determined by the following combinations of factors:

Bays.......$BBHH$ $BbHH$ $BBHh$ $BbHh$
Blacks....$bbHH$ $bbHh$
Chestnuts..$BBhh$ $Bbhh$ $bbhh$

Only the first types of bay and black breed true. Suppose, now, that the horses are mated brother with sister. From time to time, simply by chance, two animals will be mated which are homozygous in one or both of the factors. For example, two bays of formula $BbHH$ may thus be mated. Neither of them transmits the factor for chestnut (h) and it is evident that their descendants will never produce chestnuts so long as they are bred only with each other. Blacks, however, will frequently appear. These blacks, being homozygous in both factors ($bbHH$), will breed true. If brother-sister matings are made among the bays, occasionally matings of the type $BBHH$ by $BBHH$ will be made by chance, in which the factor for black is eliminated as well as that for chestnut. The descendants of this mating will be a true-breeding race of bays.

Since the unfixed matings are continually giving rise to fixed matings, while the reverse can not occur, continued inbreeding is enough to insure an automatic tendency toward fixation. This fixation of type will tend to occur even if matings are simply made at random, but will, of course, be much more rapid if accompanied by selection, that is, if bays, for example, are mated with bays only in the case above. In this simple case, selection alone will have some tendency toward fixing the bay color, but the process will be exceedingly slow. A single unfortunate mating may undo years of work. It is hardly necessary to add that the case above is so simple that any of the colors can be fixed by much more direct methods, not necessarily involving close breeding. The case is merely used to illustrate the point that inbreeding has an automatic tendency toward making all the hereditary units homozygous, or, in other words, resulting in animals which produce only one kind of reproductive cell.

A type is fixed most rapidly when matings are made between selected brothers and sisters, but the tendency toward fixation is present in almost any system of continued close breeding. There is one exception, however, which should be pointed out. The mating of sire with daughter is in a sense as close inbreeding as brother with sister. Yet a male may be bred successively with his daughters, granddaughters, great-granddaughters, etc., concentrating his blood to any extent, without coming any closer to fixing his type than at first if the type were not fixed in himself. This will be clear from an illustration. A bay stallion of formula $BbHh$ produces four kinds of reproductive cells (BH, Bh, bH, and bh). Half of these transmit the factor for black (b) and half that for chestnut (h). It is obvious that he will sire numerous black foals and chestnut foals, no matter how much his blood is concentrated. On the other hand, if it is possible to obtain a bay stallion which is known to be of formula $BBHH$, there is no quicker way of fixing a true-breeding race of bays than by repeated crosses with his female descendants. Such a stallion is prepotent, since in crosses with blacks and chestnuts he sires only bay foals.

Speaking generally, the continued use of a sire of proved prepotency is the most rapid method of fixing his type, while the use of a sire which is not prepotent has no tendency toward fixation, but rather the reverse.

ISOLATION OF GENETIC DIFFERENCES BY INBREEDING.

It was noted in the section on variation that characteristics differ greatly in the degrees to which they are determined by heredity, outside conditions which are controllable, and by uncontrollable conditions, such as chance irregularity in development. Thus, in some characteristics, such as quality of coat color and, to a less extent, type, consistent close breeding, and uniform conditions, result in a highly uniform stock. In the case of functional characteristics, especially fertility, there remains much variation even under apparently uniform conditions and any amount of inbreeding. Color pattern is also often of this kind, as we have seen in the case of guinea pigs. The Bureau of Animal Industry has a stock of guinea pigs which is descended wholly from a single mating in the twelfth generation of brother-sister mating. Variability has been reduced only 25 per cent by this inbreeding. There is still variation from nearly solid black to solid white, but none of it is now hereditary. The progeny of the blackest parents produce progeny of the same average grade as the whitest parents. Figure 9 shows the variation in pattern in four generations of guinea pigs from this inbred family.

While inbreeding is of little use in bringing about uniformity in such cases, it does something else which, perhaps, is even more important. When there is a lot of variation which is not hereditary, straight selection is especially apt to be at fault. There can be no assured progress, since a single unfortunate mating with an animal which is good by accident, not by heredity, may at any time undo all previous work. It is only by inbreeding a number of lines and comparing them that the real hereditary differences can be recognized. This was done in the inbreeding experiment with guinea pigs referred to above. Certain inbred lines averaged 15 per cent white, others 85 per cent, while others were intermediate. It is very doubtful whether the extreme types could ever have been obtained from the original stock by straight selection without close breeding. Similarly, differences in growth, fertility, and vitality were brought to light among the different families of guinea pigs. These are discussed under the next heading.

It would be difficult to overemphasize the importance of close breeding in the past history of livestock breeding, as the agent in bringing out the real hereditary differences between different stocks, and so leading to improvement in characteristics which could not have been improved by selection alone.

FIG. 9.—Four generations of inbred guinea pigs. The young pair at the right end of the line is descended from 19 generations of matings of brother with sister. Three of these generations, the parents, grandparents, and great-grandparents are in the picture. Color and other characteristics have become fixed automatically in this family because of the inbreeding. The exact coat pattern, however, as is generally the case, is not wholly determined by heredity, and is therefore unfixable.

THE EFFECT OF INBREEDING ON VIGOR.

Along with the advantages of inbreeding, certain unfortunate effects have long been known. A general reduction in vigor, especially in fertility, has long been ascribed to inbreeding, and there can be no doubt that these are common effects. It is not, however, so certain that they are invariable effects. Dr. Helen D. King, for example, has inbred rats, brother with sister, for 25 generations without any decline in size, constitutional vigor, or fertility, but rather the reverse.

The Bureau of Animal Industry has made experiments on the subject involving more than 26,000 guinea pigs. A number of distinct families have been maintained wholly by matings of brother with sister. The fact that one of these has reached the twentieth generation without any conspicuous decline in vigor in any respect is further evidence that the evils of inbreeding are by no means as great as often pictured. Other families, however, suffered a rapid decline, and some decline is shown by the average for all families. The great differences between families confirm the suggestion that inbreeding is merely likely to lead to decline in vigor, but does not necessarily do so. This conclusion is brought out also on considering the different characteristics separately. One family lost markedly in vitality but not in size or fertility. In another the reverse was the case. In fact, nearly all combinations of favorable or unfavorable characteristics were represented by one or more families after a number of generations of inbreeding.

The results of crosses between different inbred families are interesting in this connection. The young from such crosses made distinctly better gains and a larger percentage were raised of those born alive than in their inbred cousins raised at the same time under the same conditions. The crossbred females have much larger litters and have them more frequently. More of their young are born alive and the birth weights are greater than of young born of inbred dams. The second generation, in fact, appears to be as vigorous as a control stock which has never been inbred.

These results are easily interpreted by the present theory of heredity. They confirm the view that the primary effect of inbreeding is merely the automatic fixation of hereditary factors. It seems to be the usual rule that factors favorable to vigor are dominant over unfavorable ones, and hence tend to conceal the latter under crossbreeding. Under inbreeding the unfavorable factors are as likely to become fixed as favorable ones, and hence are brought to light. One or more of the unfavorable factors affecting size, vitality, or fertility are thus very likely to become fixed in each line, especially as it is very likely to happen that some of the favorable and unfavorable factors may be linked in their heredity, which means that the attempt to fix these favorable factors involves an involuntary fixation of the unfavorable ones. It usually happens that different defects become fixed in different lines, so that on crossing each supplies the elements of vigor which the other lacks and full vigor returns.

The fixation of unfavorable characteristics can be prevented to some extent by sufficiently careful selection, but it must be remembered that fertility, vigor, etc., depend on so many factors besides heredity that even the most careful selection will often be at fault. Hereditary differences in these respects can not, in fact, be determined with certainty except by starting a large number of inbred lines and comparing them. It is the discovery of one really valuable line, out of a score or more of closely bred lines, which may be expected to make history in livestock breeding.

While the conclusions in regard to inbreeding as given above are based on experiments with higher animals, it may be well to add that extensive inbreeding of insects has given similar results and that the same is true of continued self-pollination in plants as brought out by Darwin, Shull, East, Jones, and Collins and Kempton.

Summing up, the primary effect of inbreeding is the automatic fixation of some combination of hereditary factors present in a stock. This leads to uniformity of type or function, if such uniformity is possible. When not possible, owing to variability which is not genetic, the hereditary potentialities in the lines are brought out clearly, as is possible in no other way. Decline in vigor is a common but not a necessary consequence of the fixation of heredity.

CROSSBREEDING.

As inbred animals produce only one kind of reproductive cell, it is to be expected that a cross between two inbred lines will produce only one kind of progeny so far as hereditary factors are concerned. It is, in fact, well known that the first cross between two closely bred stocks is as uniform in character as either of the parent stocks. The cross between the polled black Aberdeen-Angus breed and white Shorthorns, producing polled blue roans, has already been considered. The conformation is also uniform in the first generation.

While uniform themselves, such crossbreds are anything but prepotent as breeders. When two of the above-mentioned polled blue-roan Shorthorn-Angus crosses are bred with each other, the progeny, as already mentioned, include blacks, reds, blue roans, red roans, and whites with either black or red ears. Any of the colors may be associated either with horns or polled heads. There is also increased variability in conformation.

As regards vigor and fertility, crossbreeding is likely to lead to marked improvement. As noted above, the crossing of two unrelated weakened inbred lines usually leads to a return to normal vigor.

Summing up, the first generation of a cross is as uniform in character as the parent stocks, and in general shows increased vigor. In the second generation there is increased variability, the characteristics of the grandparents being combined, as a rule, in all combinations and in all degrees.

THE SYSTEM OF BREEDING.

THE PURPOSES OF LIVESTOCK BREEDING.

Aside from mere increase in numbers, the purposes which the breeder is likely to have in mind fall under two more or less distinct heads, namely, production of a uniform product and improvement. A uniform product depends on such control over the heredity of the stock that matings can be made with the assurance that the offspring will be of a certain definite type for which there is a demand. Improvement is, of course, closely related to control over heredity, but the methods which give the greatest control are not necessarily those which lead to most rapid improvement.

UNIFORMITY OF TYPE.

The method of obtaining such uniformity of type as is possible, is, as already indicated, close breeding, accompanied by selection. This method was one of the foundations of Robert Bakewell's success in improving the Longhorn cattle and Leicestershire sheep of the eighteenth century. His example was followed in the foundation period of most of the British breeds of livestock. Injurious effects of inbreeding became apparent later in certain lines, as in the low fertility of the Bates Shorthorns. There are to-day breeders who have reached great success through inbreeding and others who have met disaster.

The degree of inbreeding which should be followed depends to a large extent on the purpose. Type, color, and utility have already been fixed to some extent in most of the pure breeds, and merely the consistent use of males of the same pure breed may be sufficiently close breeding in many cases. To fix a superior type within a breed, however, requires closer breeding. The closer the breeding, the more readily will characteristics become fixed.

The expression "line breeding" is often used for various mild forms of close breeding. Thus, continued breeding within a herd or within a few related herds, with the avoidance of close inbreeding, is a kind of line breeding. The term is perhaps most frequently used when there is an effort to concentrate the blood of an especially worthy animal by mating together animals descended from him. In either case characters are fixed more slowly than with close inbreeding. There is, in consequence, less danger of fixing undesirable qualities in the stock by accident. It may be well to add that in line breeding, as in any form of inbreeding, animals should be mated primarily on their merits, regardless of the exact degree of relationship. The attempt to follow a rigid system of mating, such as is sometimes represented on charts, usually interferes too much with selection to be a success.

The degree of inbreeding which a man can afford to follow depends in part on the size of his herd, in part on his ability in selecting the best for breeding stock, and in part on the extent to which he can take a chance. As already noted, most valuable characteristics of livestock are affected to such a large extent by feed and management and also by uncontrollable conditions, that the selection of the best individuals does not always mean selection of the best heredity. Hereditary differences can often be recognized clearly only when different inbred lines are compared with each other. Thus, among a number of inbred lines started from the same stock and maintained with equal ability, some will degenerate rapidly, the majority, perhaps, will show some unfortunate characteristic, and in only a few will the desired type become fixed in association with high vigor and fertility. Once obtained, however, the type can be kept for a long time at its high level by close breeding, and can supply prepotent males for the improvement of inferior stock.

CROSSBREEDING FOR THE MARKET.

As already noted, control over heredity, and hence uniformity, depends on the amount of close breeding back of the parents and not at all on their relationship to each other. There is no doubt, for example, that mules can be produced as true to type as any pure breed, by using closely bred jacks and mares. Experience is, of

FIG. 10.—A Poland China boar, illustrating the lard type of hog.

course, necessary to determine just what lines of jacks and mares will produce a mule of a particular size and type. It is probable that systematic crossing of breeds could be practiced to a larger extent than at present in cases in which the offspring are not to be used for breeding. An increase in vigor is to be expected. In some cases advantage can be taken of the good qualities of two breeds. The highest development of the meat type in animals is generally correlated with reduced fertility. By choosing females from a breed distinguished for its vigor and fertility, and the male from a breed of the most extreme meat type, it is possible to produce progeny of the best market type without the losses due to defective fertility.

Among hogs, Yorkshire or Tamworth sows can be used to advantage with an extreme type of Poland China or Duroc-Jersey boar. Purebred or grade Dorset ewes are useful in crosses where it is desired to produce lambs out of season. Under some circumstances dairy cows can well be bred to bulls of the beef breeds in order to produce calves which can be fattened profitably. In some cases it may even be worth while to develop races within two breeds specially designed to be complementary to each other in crosses. The danger in any system of crossbreeding is that the very excellence of the first generation will tempt the breeder to use them as breeding stock. The additional vigor due to crossing decreases after the first generation and uniformity of type is lost at once.

IMPROVEMENT.

There is a certain antagonism between control over heredity and radical improvement. Perfect control over heredity implies the absence of all variation among the progeny of a mating. A useful new type is most likely to be found where there is a maximum of variation. Thus the pioneer breeder must make wide crosses. The first generation may be expected to be about intermediate between

FIG. 11.—A group of Corriedale rams. This breed originated in Australia in the crossing of Lincoln or Leicester rams with Merino ewes. It has been developed into a true type by years of close breeding and selection.

the parents and as uniform as the uncrossed parental lines. The second generation, however, will in general show distinctly more variability. The ancestral characteristics will be found in every compatible combination and in all degrees of development if enough young are produced. Characteristics may be found which appear wholly new. If a promising new type is formed it remains to fix it by careful selection and close breeding.

There will doubtless always be room for the production of new types and from time to time even new breeds. But this work of radical improvement is not likely to occupy more than a few of the most ambitious breeders. Others will have such superior stock that they can do no better than conserve it by close breeding, making such slow improvement by selection as the limited variability of the stock permits. With a larger number, periods of close breeding must be interrupted by periods in which new blood is infused into the stock, a certain amount of uniformity being sacrificed to obtain renewed vigor and a basis for further improvement. The great body, even of the owners of purebreds, however, will own stock which is distinctly below the best of its breed. For them improvement and fixation of type can go hand in hand. The method is the consistent use of prepotent males of a given superior line.

GRADING UP.

Common stock can be improved and fixed in type by the same methods as those described last. The process in this case is known as grading up. Even two or three crosses with superior purebred

Fig. 12.—A Merino ram, an example of the fine-wool type of sheep.

males should raise the level practically to that of the average purebred, if not better, so far as individual qualities are concerned. With five or six such crosses it would doubtless be possible to produce animals better than most purebreds both in their own characteristics and in their breeding power.

It is not, however, considered practicable to permit registration of grades as purebreds, no matter how many top crosses there may be, with superior purebred males of the same breed. In all but this respect, however, a large stock of common females can be rapidly converted into a herd as good as a purebred herd by grading. It is in the grading up of the common stock of the country that scientific breeding can render its greatest service.

METHODS OF SELECTION.

GENERAL CONSIDERATIONS.

In a broad sense the whole subject of practical breeding comes under the head of selection. The considerations which should determine the general policy of mating have been discussed in the previous section.

In the present section, selection will be considered with respect to the characteristics which it is desired to improve rather than to the

FIG. 13.—A Lincoln ram, an example of the long-wool type of sheep. The Corriedale breed was developed from crosses of rams of this type with fine-wool ewes.

system of mating. The most obvious basis for such selection is the performance of the animals themselves. A dairy cow with a record of 1,000 pounds of butterfat in a year is more likely to produce a useful calf than one which produced only 200 pounds under the same circumstances. Unfortunately, the merits of most kinds of livestock can not be measured so directly. The study of conformation as an index of useful qualities has accordingly held a high place as a basis for selection of breeding stock. Livestock judging has this for its purpose. An animal of good stock is a better one to breed than one of equal individual merit but of mixed or common breeding. His prepotency is apt to be greater. The pure breeds were founded in recognition of the importance of the heredity back of the immediate parents, and pedigree, though often misused, is a valuable aid to selection, apart from its importance in following a general policy of mating. The soundest basis of all for selection of breeding stock is the record of past performance as a breeder, provided the record is sufficiently extensive to give a fair test.

The selection of the male, on whatever basis, should not depend wholly on the approximation to the ideal which the breeder has in mind, but also on the character of the females with which he is to be bred. The general rule is that the prospective sire and dam

FIG. 14.—A striking illustration of the use of a purebred sire. Two-year-old crossbred Hereford-Jersey steer, weighing 1,650 pounds, and his dam, a Jersey cow, weighing 800 pounds. The picture also illustrates the prepotency of the Hereford white face.

should be chosen so that the average of their characteristics approximates as closely as possible the ideal type. In other words, they should be alike in characteristics which are up to the standard, while defects in one should be balanced by exaggerated development in the other. This principle has special application to horse breeding in choosing the stallion to breed with a particular mare. In the case of cattle, sheep, swine, and poultry its application is necessarily more limited, as the same male can not be expected to correct the defects of all the females. In these cases the male had best approach the ideal type in all respects as closely as possible. If all the females are of the same inferior type, however, the use of a male of an exaggerated improved type may lead to most rapid progress. At one time the hogs that won the show ring awards were of an exaggerated type in which extreme early maturity went with lightness of bone, low fecundity, and excessive fatness. This show-ring type was not considered the best utility type itself, but was the best for improving the coarse, slowly maturing, common stock of that time.

INDIVIDUAL PERFORMANCE AND LIVESTOCK JUDGING.

As a general rule the most direct methods of estimating the useful qualities of animals are the most satisfactory as a basis for selection. Until relatively recently it was not practicable to make accurate tests of the milk and butterfat production of large numbers of dairy cows. The experience of dairymen with regard to the type of cow which had proved to be most productive was the best guide in selecting breeding stock. At present the records made in a cow-testing association or in attaining advanced registry in a pure breed give a direct basis for selection, and the indications from conformation are being relegated to a decidedly secondary place, although knowledge of the approved dairy conformation is still of use in picking out the more promising cows from common stock or from among untested purebreds.

Similarly, the trap-nest record is coming to be more important in finding the best egg-laying strains of poultry than the approach to a standard type. Wool production is of course judged directly. Among Standardbred trotters and pacers speed, of course, has been the all-important qualification from the first and has been fixed much better than conformation. During the longer history of the English Thoroughbred both speed and conformation have been fixed to a greater extent than in the Standardbred, but the prime basis for selection has always been success on the race course. The judging of heavy horses by conformation and action is probably as direct as is practicable. In the meat breeds of cattle, swine, sheep, and poultry study of the conformation gives the best indication of the actual quantity and quality of the meat which can be got without killing the animal and also gives indications as to early maturity. Detailed descriptions of the approved types can be found in bulletins on the various breeds of livestock.

There are constant attempts to find a short cut to correct judgment through a correlation between some easily observed characteristic and the useful qualities. The development of the so-called escutcheon of dairy cattle was at one time very widely accepted as an indication of milking capacity, although the supposed correlation appears to have no basis in fact. In the case of poultry there are a number of ways, without taking trap-nest records, of picking out the hens which have been laying consistently. In breeds with yellow shanks those with the palest color have been proved to be the better layers. This is, however, really a more direct test than it seems. since the yellow color of the yolk of the egg is the same as that in the skin. In times of heavy laying the yellow coloring matter from green feed is taken up by the eggs instead of by the skin. Other tests, such as those depending on the spread of the pelvic bones or the time of molting, are even more direct.

There is another class of indirect indications of utility which should be mentioned. There is no reason for believing that the white face of the Hereford has any physiological connection with profitable meat production. The breeders of Hereford cattle, however, fixed this characteristic at the same time that they were fixing a good beef type. As it has been fixed in no other breed of cattle, it is a valuable indication of Hereford breeding when found in common stock. Conversely, fancy points which are lost on crossing have value as indications of pure breeding.

THE BREEDING RECORD.

The most direct evidence of the value of an animal in breeding, of course, is the past record in this respect. The discovery of prepotent animals of a desirable kind means more for breed progress than any other factor. It is only necessary to recall the influence of Hambletonian 10 and his son, George Wilkes, on the American trotter, of De Kol 2d on the Holstein-Friesian cattle of this country, and of Anxiety 4th on American Herefords. In judging the value of an animal on this basis the number of his progeny and the character of the animals with which he or she was mated must, of course, be taken into account. Uniform excellence in all of a large number of progeny outweighs a record of one champion among many culls.

This method of selection is, of course, more applicable to males than to females, since the latter seldom have offspring enough until quite old. Unfortunately, it is very common to dispose of males before their value as sires is established, largely because of fear of inbreeding. There is probably nothing which will make for progress more than a systematic recording of the breeding record of promising sires, such as we have in the advanced registry for dairy bulls, based on the performance of their daughters.

PEDIGREE.

The ancestry of an animal as a clue to his probable success as an individual and as a breeder should first be considered as a whole. It makes a great deal of difference whether he is purebred, high-grade, crossbred, half-blood, or merely scrub. If there is line breeding to some prepotent individual and the other ancestors for several generations indicate consistent selection toward the same type, it is very likely both that the animal will himself develop into this type and that he will be markedly prepotent. On the other hand, an array of ancestors of varied types, even though each is among the best of its kind, indicates an animal about which little can be predicted as to his own performance and less as to his progeny.

The value of particular individuals in the pedigree depends on the degree of relationship. A noteworthy sire or dam is a very important consideration. A noteworthy great-grandsire does not mean much by himself, and the more remote ancestors hardly need be taken into account as individuals.

Attention should also be paid to collateral relatives. Each full brother or sister counts as much as a parent. Half brothers and sisters and full brothers and sisters of the parents are as closely related as grandparents. First cousins are related as closely as great-grandparents.

If the past breeding record of an individual is a better indication of his future success than his pedigree, it follows that in judging the value of a pedigree the breeding record of the sire is more important than his ancestry. The breeding record of the dam is important as

FIG. 15.—Yearling Shorthorn bull.

far as it goes, but may not be extensive enough to have much weight. The breeding record of her sire is likely to give more information. Thus, the worth and similarity in type of the progeny produced by the three or four closest top-cross males in the ancestry, in connection with their own worth and their relationship to one another, are the most important considerations in passing judgment on a pedigree. About twice as much weight should be given to the sire as to the dam's sire, and so on.

In judging the value of a pedigree, it is, of course, important to give as much weight to the inferior animals represented as to the champions. Unfortunately, it is not possible to learn much of the characteristics of any but the latter class. The rest of the pedigree consists merely of names. A knowledge of the methods and ideals of the leading breeders is of great assistance in giving substance to these names.

Pedigree of Roan Gauntlet.

ROAN GAUNTLET 45276 (35284).
- Royal Duke of Gloster 20901 (28864).
  - Grand Duke of Gloster 19900 (26288).
    - *Champion of England (17526).
      - Lancaster Comet (11663)
      - Virtue
    - Duchess of Gloster 9th.
      - †Lord Raglan (13244)
      - Duchess of Gloster 6th
  - Mimulus.
    - *Champion of England (17526).
      - Lancaster Comet (11663)
      - Virtue
    - Mistletoe.
      - †Lord Raglan (13244)
      - Maidstone
- Princess Royal.
  - *Champion of England (17526).
    - Lancaster Comet (11663)
    - Virtue
  - Carmine.
    - The Czar (20947).
      - Plantagenet (11906)
      - Verdant
    - Cressida.
      - †Lord Raglan (13244)
      - Corianda
    - John Bull (11618)
    - Clipper

ROAN GAUNTLET 45276 (35284).

DAM.

Princess Royal.
Carmine.
Cressida.
Clipper.

SIRE.

Royal Duke of Gloster 20901 (28864).
Champion of England (17526).
The Czar (20947).
John Bull (11618).
Billy (3151).

It is evident from what has been said that it is an exceedingly difficult thing to be able to judge quickly and accurately the amount which a certain pedigree adds to or subtracts from the value of an animal as an individual. A very detailed knowledge of breed history, recent and past, is necessary, as well as good judgment. The past history can be learned in part from standard books on the breeds, while the recent history, which is more important, can be best acquired by following the results at the great shows and sales for a few years and keeping in touch with the current breed journals. The pedigree of any purebred can easily be obtained from the herd, flock, or studbook.

The best method of writing a pedigree for the purpose of study is that given for Amos Cruikshank's famous Shorthorn bull, Roan Gauntlet, in the tabulation shown. All the ancestors for a number of generations are shown in their proper relations to each other. Any line breeding in the pedigree is at once brought out. In the case of Roan Gauntlet the accompanying form shows that he traces in every line to a mating of Mr. Cruikshank's great bull, Champion of England, with a daughter or granddaughter of Lord Raglan.

The other common method of writing pedigrees is given for Roan Gauntlet below the full tabulation. The dam, her dam, and so on in the straight female line, are named in the first column. Opposite each female is written the name of her sire. It is very common in this form to add the name of the breeder after each animal, a practice which, as already noted, is often of value in giving significance to otherwise unknown names. To the breeder who is thoroughly acquainted with the leading sires in his breed, their own merit and that of their progeny, the names of the three or four males at the top of the column may be sufficient for a very satisfactory estimate of the value of the pedigree. Unfortunately, this form of pedigree is likely to lead to undue weight being placed on the female line of ancestry. Owing to their smaller numbers, the sires are in general superior to the dams both in breeding and as individuals. Thus the straight female line is apt to be the weakest in the whole pedigree. Direction of attention to this line has merely the somewhat negative justification that if it is good the whole pedigree is likely to be good.

The amount of information necessary for weighing properly the value of a pedigree is so great that a large number of men arrive at their conclusions by some short cut. The usual short cut in this case is the basing of values on family names, assigned to animals in a more or less arbitrary way. If the families really represented closely bred lines—breeds within breeds—this would be satisfactory, but that is seldom the case. In some breeds, the family name applies to all the descendants through the straight female line from some particular female. The second form of pedigree described above has the unfortunate effect of appearing to sanction this system. After a few generations such a family name may mean practically nothing as regards either type or breeding. A judgment based on a family name in the straight male line is no better. The direction of attention away from real values always means deterioration in the end. A fancy for a particular name thus tends to correct itself in the long run, but may work great harm to a breed in the meantime.

THE VALUE OF PUREBREDS.

The characteristics of our domestic animals are the result of a very gradual evolution, which has taken place in the course of centuries. Even our average scrubs are doubtless superior, in their usefulness to man, to the wild animals from which they are remotely descended. Until quite recently most of this improvement probably came about rather in spite of, than because of, the current beliefs in regard to heredity; one sound principle, the selection of the best for breeding, was, however, widely enough applied to bring about a slow progress. That our livestock are on the average still far from utilizing their feedstuffs to the greatest advantage in producing food, clothing, and work is shown by the achievements of individual animals, usually belonging to one or another of the pure breeds. These pure breeds are the tangible result of a century and a half of conscious effort at improvement. As hope for a more satisfactory livestock situation in the country depends on the further improvement of pure breeds and on the diffusion of their influence through the common stock, it will be well to consider briefly what has already been accomplished.

The value of the purebreds is clearest in those cases in which the capability of the animals is measured most directly. No one would question, for example, the supremacy of the English Thoroughbred in speed and gameness, a supremacy gained by a long period of the most direct selection. Among the farm animals, the best illustration can be found in dairy cattle, although careful yearly tests of milk and butterfat production are relatively recent affairs. The enormous differences among dairy cows when given the same opportunity have been brought out clearly in a great number of cases. Careful studies have shown that these differences are strongly inherited through both the sire and the dam. The average for purebreds and grades is also much above that for the average milk cow of the United States, which produces only about 4,000 pounds of milk and 160 pounds of butterfat in a year.

DAIRY CATTLE.

The great improvement which can be made by better feeding and by the grading up of common cows by the use of purebred sires has been demonstrated in all the many cases to which the writer has seen reference. Since, however, it is not possible in most cases to separate clearly the effects of grading up from those of better feeding and management, it may be well to refer briefly to an experiment recently reported by McCandlish, Gillette, and Kildee, of the Iowa agricultural experiment station, in which this can be done.

A number of scrub milk cows were brought to the station from a region of Arkansas in which purebred bulls had not been used. Their average milk production was not known but was doubtless much less than that which was obtained from the same cows under careful

FIG. 16.—A Guernsey bull of excellent type.

management at the station. Five of the cows were mature, 2 were 4 years old, and 7 either were very young heifers when obtained or were born at the station. These scrubs were bred to purebred bulls (Holstein, Guernsey, and Jersey), none of which were high priced. The records, all made under the same conditions, may be summarized as follows, after making the proper correction for age:

Effect of breeding scrub milk cows to purebred bulls.

Description.	Cows tested.	Lactation periods.	Average pounds milk.	Average pounds butterfat.
Scrubs—mature when obtained	5	15	3,169	154
Scrubs—4 years old when obtained	2	15	3,598	166
Scrubs—developed at station	7	28	4,036	191
One-half pure blood	13	40	5,556	253
Three-fourths pure blood	5	6	8,402	358

RESULTS OF IOWA EXPERIMENT IN GRADING UP SCRUB DAIRY STOCK.

The table indicates that a heifer which has developed under favorable conditions will produce more milk than one which did not have this advantage (increase of 27 per cent in milk, 24 per cent in butterfat). The most important thing brought out, however, is the great improvement made by one cross with purebred sires (38 per cent in milk production, 32 per cent in butterfat). The data for three-quarter bloods are rather meager, but show such a very great increase that it can be hardly doubted that a substantial increase over the first cross will be shown when larger numbers are available. When each of the grade cows is compared with her scrub dam or granddam, the improvement appears even more striking, owing to the fact that some of the dams were in the group of scrubs which were mature when brought to the station. Considerable difference was found in the value of the different bulls used. One of them produced hardly any improvement in his daughters, while others were responsible for a big increase in production.

It is important to understand the essential difference between a good and a poor producer. An investigation by C. H. Eckles, of the University of Missouri, brought out no important differences in the quantity of feed used by the cows merely in maintaining their weight when dry, nor in the amount of milk and butter produced by a given amount of additional feed. The good producer merely ate more feed in addition to the maintenance ration than the poor producer. This does not mean that a better appetite is the cause of higher production. The situation is probably the reverse. It shows, however, that the greater economy of high producers lies in the smaller percentage of their feed used for mere maintenance. The average cow, producing 160 pounds of butterfat a year, eats about 50 per cent more than if she were dry. Her milk scarcely pays for her keep. A cow which eats 100 per cent more than her maintenance requirements should produce twice as much milk as the former cow, with only one-third more feed. If the average American cow were of the latter kind, producing about 320 pounds of butterfat in a year, only half as many cows would be needed as at present and only two-thirds as much feed would be consumed in producing our present milk supply. With still more productive cows, milk can be produced still more cheaply, although it should be said that the rate of decline in feed cost decreases rapidly for production above 320 pounds. As a very considerable number of cows, including representatives of all the important breeds, have records of 900 pounds of butterfat in a year, the attainment of an average of 320 pounds is not a very ambitious undertaking.

As for the breeds of dairy cows, each has its advantages. The Jerseys and Guernseys, for example, produce richer milk than the Holstein-Friesians, but on the average less of it. The average difference in butterfat production, relative to the size of the animals and their cost of upkeep, is probably not very great. The differences between good and poor strains within each breed are much more important than differences between two breeds.

QUALITY IN MEAT.

The world-wide trend toward a falling per capita production of meat and the rising prices relative to other foods make the more economical production of meat a pressing problem. Both better methods of management and the improvement of the native stock by grading are of the greatest importance in this connection. The differences between purebred and scrub stock and the advantages to be expected by the grading up of the latter, however, are often misunderstood. The improvement is not primarily in size or even in the apparent economy of gains. The three most important breeds of beef cattle—Shorthorn, Hereford, and Aberdeen Angus— are indeed of large size, and when crossed with scrub beef cows or with milk cows which are undersized by heredity and not merely stunted by lack of proper feeding, they produce great improvement in this respect. Shorthorn and Hereford bulls have done wonders for the western range cattle in this way as well as in others. The pure breeds of swine and the larger breeds of sheep have also often been used to advantage to increase the size of native stock. There are, however, many large-sized scrubs.

The Holstein-Friesian cattle probably have the largest bony framework of all the breeds, but are not the best beef cattle. Feeding tests at experiment stations have often shown very little difference in either rate or gain or the cost per pound of gain when purebred or high-grade beef steers were compared with steers of scrub or dairy breeding. Holstein-Friesian steers, as might be expected, have shown up especially well in such tests. Similar results have been obtained in comparing purebred swine with "razorbacks" raised under the same conditions.

In the tests with cattle, however, the animals of beef type and breeding usually finished out into a class for which the market would pay considerably more than for the finished scrub or dairy steers. The per cent which the dressed weight forms of the live weight depends largely on the degree of fattening, and varies from 40 per cent in thin cows to 70 in the most highly finished steers. Under the same conditions steers of beef breeding usually dress out from 1 to 5 per cent more than common or dairy steers. There is also a slight difference in the size of the cuts from different parts of the carcass. Nature tends to develop most flesh in the muscles which do the most work. In the beef breeds of cattle, animals have been selected for breeding in which there was as much flesh as possible in the little-used muscles of the back and loin. The high-priced cuts from the back and loin, in fact, do form a slightly larger percentage of the dressed weight in beef steers than in common ones. The greater value of the meat from steers of beef breeding is largely, however, ascribed to the somewhat elusive element quality.

If the greater use of purebred bulls is merely to improve the average quality of beef and not to increase the quantity produced in the country with a given consumption of feed, it may seem to be of no very great importance. It appears, however, that in this case superior quality really means greater food value. The essential differences between a beef steer and the average scrub are probably

FIG. 17.—Aberdeen-Angus steer of excellent beef type.

brought out most thoroughly in an experiment by Dr. H. P. Armsby and J. A. Fries (Bureau of Animal Industry Bulletin 128).

An Aberdeen-Angus steer was fed in comparison with a scrub. The utilization of the feed was investigated by the most thorough methods. In agreement with the usual results, there was little difference in gains or cost per pound of gain. The beef steer dressed out better—60 per cent compared with 54.5 per cent—and the loin formed 17.5 per cent of the dressed weight, compared with 16.4 per cent in the scrub, which had more weight in the cheaper cuts. The beef steer, though greater in height and length of body at a year of age, was reached or passed by the scrub later in those respects. The beef steer, however, greatly surpassed the scrub in girth of body. Evidently the scrub continued growing for a longer time in bone and muscle, while the purebred, after a more rapid early growth, matured earlier and turned to fattening with greater facility. There was an important difference in the amount of feed just necessary to keep the animals from losing weight, the scrub requiring about 19 per cent more feed for this purpose. The purebred, moreover, was able to consume and utilize a larger amount of concentrated feed above his maintenance requirement than the scrub, the same difference, it will be recalled, as that between a good and a poor dairy cow.

These advantages may appear impossible to reconcile with the lack of difference in gains or cost per pound of gain. The explanation is that the purebred packed more food value into a pound of gain. A pound of his meat contained a great deal more fat and

Fig. 18.—Yorkshire boar, illustrating the bacon type of hog.

practically as much protein, but very much less water. Thus a pound of meat from the purebred was not merely of higher quality, because of the superior marbling with fat, but really contained 40 per cent more food value. Thus under the same conditions a pound of meat from a properly finished purebred is no more comparable with a pound from a scrub than is a pound of rich milk with a pound of low-testing milk.

Thus the important qualities which breeders have developed in the breeds of beef cattle are the blocky conformation with the greatest development of the more valuable cuts and the smallest amount of waste; the low maintenance requirement which results from a placid disposition; the rapid but soon completed growth in bone and muscle, in which large size is combined with early maturity; and, finally, ease of fattening.

The improved breeds of hogs have a similar advantage over scrubs in conformation, disposition, early maturity, and ease of fattening, resulting in the production of a more concentrated food product at no more or at less cost per pound. The hog, however, has such an

FIG. 19.—A Piney-Woods ewe.

excessive tendency to fatten that the most improved breeds do not produce the best quality of meat. They are valuable, primarily, for the lard which they produce. The breeds with more vigorous

FIG. 20.—First cross between a Piney-Woods ewe and a purebred ram, showing improvement in type and wool.

growth and less tendency to fatten, such as the Tamworth and Yorkshire, produce a better quality of ham and bacon.

In parts of the Corn Belt the native hogs have been improved to such extent by crosses with purebreds that the advantages of consistent grading to one pure breed are perhaps rather in obtaining uniformity of color and type than in efficiency of pork production. In many parts of the country, however, there is still much room for improvement in the fundamental qualities.

Sheep breeding is complicated by the simultaneous selection for wool and mutton. Each of the breeds produces its own characteristic kind of wool. Any desired fineness or length of fiber which is found in a pure breed can easily be fixed in common stock by grading up. As regards mutton, the same principles apply as in beef production. The same qualities have been fixed in the middle and long-wool breeds of sheep as in the beef breeds of cattle.

FIG. 21.—The same Piney-Woods ewe as in figure 19, showing the lack of wool on the abdomen. Total wool clip, 3 pounds.

FIG. 22.—First cross between Piney-Woods ewe and a purebred ram, showing wool on abdomen. Total clip, 8 pounds.

BREEDING AND SOUNDNESS IN HORSES.

The hereditary differences among the breeds of horses are more conspicuous than in any other kind of livestock. Differences in weight, speed, and conformation are fairly well fixed in the pure breeds, but, of course, unfixed in scrubs. The effect of a cross with a given pure breed can be predicted, at least in a rough way, but no predictions are of value in case the stallion is a scrub. Of the greatest importance for any kind of horse are good feet and legs. Scrub stallions, even if apparently sound themselves, are more likely to transmit unsoundness than stallions of the pure breeds, especially if the latter are known to come from sound stock. There is, perhaps, less excuse for scrub stallions than for scrub males of any other kind of livestock.

Whether it is advisable for a man who breeds only 1 or 2 mares a year to breed always to a stallion of the same pure breed is more often questioned. It may seem best to attempt to balance a certain defect in a grade Percheron mare by breeding to a Clydesdale stallion. The colt is practically a crossbred and should have the vigor of a crossbred with at least the general conformation and size of a draft horse. There is, however, much more uncertainty in such breeding than in consistent grading to a single pure breed. In crossbreeding,

FIG. 21.—A Percheron stallion.

Descendant of a long line of impressive ancestors and himself a sire of valuable draft horses.

one defect on which attention is fixed may be improved, but unexpected ones are likely to appear. In shifting constantly from breed to breed there can be no assured progress toward a definite ideal.

POULTRY.

The various breeds of standardbred poultry have been selected in the past largely according to type and feathers. The heavy breeds can be trusted to excel in meat production, but the situation has not been very satisfactory in regard to eggs. With the systematic taking of yearly egg records, however, it will probably not be long before reliable strains of egg producers will have become thoroughly established in all the breeds with pretensions in this direction. Great differences among breeds and strains within the breeds have been clearly demonstrated.

SATISFACTION FROM PLEASING APPEARANCE.

In this discussion, attention has been devoted in the main to the strictly practical merits of the pure breeds. It would not be fair to

FIG. 24.—A Standardbred stallion.

conclude without referring to another aspect. This is the satisfaction to be derived from a uniform stock which presents a pleasing appearance in type and color. The appeal of the beautiful or majestic in livestock has been, perhaps, the most important motive leading to their improvement. Pride in the possession of such livestock and the constant inspiration to be derived from their further improvement are considerations beyond the purely material advantages.

FIG. 25.—Typical results of grading up with poultry. A, standardbred Barred Plymouth Rock male; B, mongrel hen: C, grade hen (½ blood); D, grade hen (¾ blood); E, grade hen (⅞ blood); F, grade cock (⅞ blood).

SUMMARY.

Animals and plants are composed of microscopical units—the cells. Each cell has a specialized central portion, the nucleus, which contains a number of threadlike or rodlike bodies called chromosomes. The number of chromosomes is constant in each kind of animal or plant.

Every animal begins its career in the union of two cells—the egg cell from the dam and the sperm from the sire.

In a sense the reproductive cells are not produced by the parents but are unspecialized bits of the same material from which the parents themselves originally developed. Heredity consists merely in the retention, by the reproductive cells, of the power to develop into a complete individual under the proper conditions.

Characteristics acquired by the parents through training, care, or accident are not transmitted to their progeny. Belief in the influences of telegony and maternal impressions has no scientific foundation.

The heredity, transmitted by the reproductive cells, is composed of unit factors, each of which is handed on unchanged from generation to generation.

Hereditary differences depend on the existence of alternative forms of certain unit factors. Such alternative factors are called allelomorphs of each other.

The egg and sperm each contain, typically, a full set of the unit factors characteristic of the kind of animal. Their union results in a double set in the fertilized egg.

This double set may be composed in part of pairs of identical factors and in part of pairs of alternative factors. The individual is said to be homozygous in regard to the former, and heterozygous in regard to the latter.

It often happens that one of the alternative factors in a heterozygous individual expresses itself fully in development at the expense of the other. Such a factor is said to be dominant. The factor whose influence is suppressed is said to be recessive. The normal type of a species is usually dominant over deviations from normal.

Most characteristics depend on the combined influence of a number of pairs of factors.

The double set of factors in the individual is sorted out into single sets in the formation of the reproductive cells. Individuals produce only one kind of reproductive cell in those respects in which they are homozygous and two kinds in those in which they are heterozygous.

Parallel to the results of genetic experiments, the microscope reveals the chromosomes in pairs in the body cells, in place of the single set to be observed in the reproductive cells. There is convincing evidence that the chromosomes are the bearers of the hereditary factors.

In most cases two factors which come into an individual's heredity from the same parent are no more likely to go into the same reproductive cell than two factors which were derived from opposite parents.

In some cases, on the other hand, there is a tendency for factors which enter a cross together to come out together in the second generation. Such factors are said to be linked with each other in inheritance.

The hereditary factors of a species fall into groups in such a manner that those in the same group are all linked with one another, while those in different groups show no linkage. It is believed that each linkage group contains the factors which are carried by a given chromosome.

Sex is normally determined by a difference in the chromosomes. In some cases, including mammals, the male produces two kinds of sperms, male and female determining, respectively. In other cases, including birds, it is the female that is heterozygous for sex.

A number of characteristics are known which are linked with sex in inheritance in such way as to indicate that they are carried by the chromosome that determines sex.

No practical means of modifying the sex ratio is yet known, with the possible exception of inbreeding and selection.

The colors of farm livestock depend in most cases on relatively few unit factors. The same is true of a few other characteristics, such as the polled condition of cattle and the various comb shapes of poultry.

Differences in size, type, and function are believed to depend in most cases on many factors. Their inheritance can not, so far as known at present, be controlled by such direct methods as the simpler characteristics.

There is equal inheritance from the sexes.

Prepotency depends neither on breed nor on sex, nor does the prepotency of an individual in one respect indicate his prepotency in others. In part, prepotency depends on the nature of the heredity back of particular characteristics, especially on the dominance of the factors which are involved. In part, it depends on the fixation of heredity, which means the making of all pairs of factors homozygous.

Variation is composed of four elements: that due to different combinations of hereditary factors, that due to the appearance of new hereditary factors (or mutations), that due to outside conditions which can be controlled, and that due to uncontrollable conditions, such as chance irregularity in development. Some characteristics are determined to a greater degree by heredity than others.

Straight selection is sometimes effective in fixing characters, but a single unfortunate cross is likely at any time to upset much previous work.

The primary effect of inbreeding is the automatic fixation of some combination of hereditary factors present in the stock. This leads to uniformity of type or function, if such uniformity is possible. When not possible, owing to variation which is not genetic, the hereditary potentialities of different lines are at least clearly brought out. Decline in vigor is a common but not a necessary consequence of the fixation of heredity.

The first generation of a cross is as uniform in character as the parent stocks, and, in general, shows increased vigor. The type is usually, but not always, intermediate between that of the parents. In the second generation there is increased variability, the characteristics of the grandparents being combined, as a rule, in all combinations and degrees.

Aside from mere increase in numbers, the principal objects of breeding are to produce uniformity of a desired type and improvement.

Uniformity of type depends on close breeding accompanied by selection, and may either be fixed within a line or secured in the first generation of a cross.

Radical improvement depends on crossbreeding followed by close breeding and selection in order to fix the desired combination of characteristics when obtained.

Improvement of inferior types, whether scrub or purebred, depends on the consistent use of prepotent males of the same breed or line within the bred.

Selection of breeding stock requires good judgment in estimating the merits and properly weighing the claims of the animal's performance, his conformation, pedigree, and previous success as a breeder.

The most direct tests of performance are the best.

The best evidence of the value of an animal in breeding is his past record in this respect, if sufficiently extensive.

In judging the value of a pedigree, the worth and similarity in type of the progeny produced by the three or four closest top-cross males in the ancestry in connection with their own worth and their relationship to one another are the most important considerations. The sire should be given twice as much weight as the dam's sire, and so on.

The pure breeds of livestock are the successful results of past efforts at improvement and should form the basis for further progress.

Made in the USA
Coppell, TX
19 September 2020

38419599R00044